A Classic Tale of Sport and Mysticism

"Golf is of games the most mystical, the least earthbound, the one wherein the walls between us and the supernatural are rubbed thinnest. There is much wit and good will in *Golf in the Kingdom*."
—John Updike, *The New Yorker*

"This is a Western equivalent of Herrigel's famous *Zen in the Art of Archery*, but a much better book, in which a sport is employed as a yoga or spiritual discipline. Furthermore, the writing is so fine that one can smell the heather and the whiskey and feel the intense human warmth of all the characters involved."   —Alan Watts

". . . a high-flying, metaphysical exercise that might be called a contemporary, Merion-blue-grass version of *Sartor Resartus*. . . Murphy writes with a fine knowledge of golf and with style and humor, and *Golf in the Kingdom* may very well be the best 'serious' golf book since Arnold Haultain's *The Mystery of Golf* in 1908."
—Herbert Warren Wind

". . . a peculiarly charming story"
—Christopher Lehmann-Haupt, *The New York Times*

"*Golf in the Kingdom* reveals, beyond every doubt, the connection between sport and the higher realms of mysticism."
—George Leonard

An Esalen Book

The Esalen Publishing Program is edited by Stuart Miller

PENGUIN

ARKANA

GOLF IN THE KINGDOM

Michael Murphy, a native Californian, founded the Esalen Institute (with Richard Price)
in 1962. A graduate of Stanford University, he
did further work there in philosophy and spent
a year and a half at the Sri Aurobindo Ashram
in Pondicherry, India. He is also the author of
Jacob Atabet, *An End to Ordinary History*, and
The Future of the Body.

"Hell," from *The Garden of Earthly Delights* by Hieronymus Bosch. Shivas Irons claimed that Bosch played an early form of golf called *kolven*. This painting, he said, depicts the agonies the painter saw on those early golf courses.

Golf in the Kingdom

Michael Murphy

ARKANA

ARKANA BOOKS
Published by the Penguin Group
Penguin Books USA Inc.,
375 Hudson Street, New York, New York 10014, U.S.A.
Penguin Books Ltd, 27 Wrights Lane, London W8 5TZ, England
Penguin Books Australia Ltd, Ringwood, Victoria, Australia
Penguin Books Canada Ltd, 10 Alcorn Avenue,
Toronto, Ontario, Canada M4V 3B2
Penguin Books (N.Z.) Ltd, 182–190 Wairau Road,
Auckland 10, New Zealand

Penguin Books Ltd, Registered Offices:
Harmondsworth, Middlesex, England

First published in the United States of America by
The Viking Press, Inc., 1972
Published in Arkana 1992

15 14 13 12 11 10

An Esalen Book

LIBRARY OF CONGRESS CATALOGING IN PUBLICATION DATA
Murphy, Michael, 1930 Sept. 3–
Golf in the Kingdom/Michael Murphy.
p.   cm.
Includes bibliographical references.
ISBN 0 14 019.450 9
1. Golf—Psychological aspects.   2. Occultism.   I. Title.
GV979.P75M8   1992
796.352′01—dc20   91-32443

Printed in the United States of America

For my parents,
John and Marie Murphy

*"The game was invented a billion years ago—
don't you remember?"*

—Old Scottish golf saying

Contents

Golf in the Kingdom

PART I

Shivas Irons

In Scotland, between the Firth of Forth and the Firth of Tay, lies the Kingdom of Fife—known to certain lovers of that land simply as "The Kingdom." There, on the shore of the North Sea, lies a golfing links that shimmers in my memory— an innocent stretch of heather and grassy dunes that cradled the unlikely events which grew into this book. For reasons political and arcane I cannot tell you its real name, so will call it instead the Links of Burningbush. Maybe you have played it yourself and will recognize it from my description. But I must warn you that even its terrain and the name of the town in which it is located are veiled, for the members of the venerable golf club that governs those links are strangely threatened by the story I will tell.

There I met Shivas Irons, introduced to me simply as a golf professional, by accident one day in June 1956. I played a round of golf with him then, joined him in a gathering of friends that evening, followed him into a ravine at midnight looking for his mysterious teacher, watched him go into ecstatic trance as the sun came up, and left for London the following afternoon—just twenty-four hours after we had met—shaken, exalted, my perception of things permanently altered.

The first part of this book is about that incredible day, seen again through fifteen years in which my memory of our meeting passed through unaccountable changes. How did he and his teacher carry on their experiments with consciousness and the structure of space during all those rounds of golf on the Burningbush Links without the players or green-keepers ever knowing? Did he actually change shape and size as I seem to remember him doing, or was that a result of the traumas I went through then? Did he drive the eighteenth green some 320 yards away? I'm fairly certain he did that. During the years since our meeting I have been haunted by questions like these. Our day together has gotten into my inner life, shaping and reshaping my memories, my attitudes, my perceptions. At times I almost think he is here in the flesh, his presence is so vivid, especially when I play a round of golf. Then I could swear he is striding down the fairways with me, admonishing or consoling me with that resonant Scottish burr or suggesting some subtle readjust-ment of my swing. His haunting presence leads me back to the game, in spite of all my prejudice against its apparent inanities. On a golf course I can begin to recreate that day in 1956.

Part two of this book is my attempt to make sense of some passages which I was fortunate enough to copy from his journals. For the man was a philosopher-poet and an historian of sorts. His sayings have stuck in my mind as well as the memory of his prodigious golf shots. Whatever led me to copy those sentences escapes me now. Like my meeting with him, I must put it down to unbelievably good luck. Or perhaps I knew, in some precognitive way, that I was not to see him again. For I have tried without success these several years to re-establish contact with him. In the town of Burningbush no one knows where he is or what he is doing. He is simply—as the barman at the ancient golf club said—at large in the world.

When I left Scotland after that memorable visit, I was on my way to India, to study philosophy and practice meditation at the ashram of the Indian seer Aurobindo. When I reached my destination, I became absorbed in the discipline I found there and the memory of my time in Burningbush began to recede. In that austere and devoted place adventures on golf courses seemed a frivolous waste of time. My rhetoric and interior dialogues then were clothed in the words of Aurobindo and Saint John of the Cross, Plotinus and Meister Eckhart. Hardly a notion or phrase from my conversations in Scotland crept in.

After a year and a half in India, I returned to California. It was then that Shivas Irons began to haunt me. I began to hear his voice, making the same suggestions he had made to me during our day together. "Aye one fiedle afore ye e'er swung," the sentence came like a litany. Sometimes I would hear him as I was falling asleep.

In the summer of 1961 Richard Price, a classmate from Stanford who had become fascinated with the latent possibilities of the mind, heard that I was living in San Francisco and came to see me. Before long we had conceived a plan for an institute in Big Sur, on my family's old estate there, and our dream soon became a reality of sorts—not the one we had talked about exactly, but something like it, something recognizably in the direction of an ashram and forum where East and West could meet. About that time memories of Shivas took an even stronger hold on me. That someone so mystically gifted should be a golf professional— and such a proficient one—filled me with increasing wonder. For the difficulties of remembering and embodying the higher life while laboring in the lower were becoming ever more apparent as our little institute took shape. Psychiatrists, hippies, and swingers, learned men from universities and research centers, wounded devoted couples and gurus from the end of the world were descending upon us in answer to our letters and brochures. We were caught in a social movement we hardly knew existed. New adventures of the spirit were beginning, of the spirit and the body, of the spirit and the bedroom, of encounter groups and endless therapies—a vast exploration of what my teacher Aurobindo had called "the vital nature." Swept along in the heady river of The Human Potential, as we called it then, I came to admire what Shivas Irons had so firmly joined in his life—all those worlds above and below that met in his remarkable golf swing, in the way he greeted friends at the bar of the Burningbush club.

One night in Big Sur, after a particularly rousing and exhausting session of something called "psychological karate," I was drawn to the box of papers I had collected during my trip to India. I found the notes I had copied from his journals. Seeing them again in Big Sur, so far from the Kingdom of Fife, brought back the experience like a flood. Suddenly the feeling of it all, the smell of heather and those evanescent vistas of purple and green were there again in all their original intensity. For an hour or so I was in Scotland again, walking the cobblestone streets of that little town, smelling the salt air, looking out in some kind of satori from the hill above hole thirteen. The thrill of it was so deep, so full of blazing awareness that I wondered how I-had forgotten. I was dumfounded, as I read through those notes, at my genius for repression.

I decided that the time had come to reestablish contact. The next day I wrote him a letter. Months passed without a reply. But my desire to hear from him continued to grow. I wrote a second letter sometime during the summer of 1964, but still there was no reply. I wrote a third to his friends the McNaughtons, but it was returned without a forwarding address. By then it was well into 1965 and I was caught up in the full tide of those utopian days at our institute. We were becoming famous, at least in certain circles, and for a while it seemed that we were on the verge of some immense discovery. We were planning a Residential Program with a huge array of disciplines for stretching the human potential; the idea behind it was to develop "astronauts of inner space" who would break through to dimensions of consciousness not yet explored by the human race. At times we talked in terms of a "Manhattan Project" of the psyche. But it soon became evident that breakthroughs could be in the wrong direction, that we were in for a longer haul than some of us had thought. Our more ambitious programs began to founder as some of our astronauts came crashing back to earth, and we began to learn that the programing of consciousness was an unpredictable venture. This sobering change in perspective was reinforced by what we saw happening in the Big Sur country around us. Thousands of young people from all over the United States were coming down the coast highway looking for some final Mecca of the counter-culture, and during the summer of 1967, the "Summer of Love," it seemed that most of them wanted to camp on our grounds. They came with dazed and loving looks, with drugs and fires, swarming into the redwood canyons and up over the great coast ridges, many of them polluting and stealing along the way. The air was filled with a drunken mysticism that undermined every discipline we set for the place. Late that summer I got hepatitis.

Convalescing, I resolved that I would visit Burningbush again and find the man who embodied so much of the life I was aspiring for, so much that was lacking in that summer of chaos. But a slow recovery and the adventures and problems of our institute kept me from the journey for another three years. I was not able to arrange a visit until the summer of 1970.

I had come to England with a group of friends, and as soon as I could I rented a car and drove to Edinburgh, and thence to the Kingdom of Fife. But what disappointment! Shivas was long gone, where he was no one knew. His old landlady rolled back her eyes when I asked about him, gave a wistful shrug, and said that letters sent to his forwarding address in London were now returned. He had left sometime in the fall of 1963. "Oh, he was a wild one," she said in that fondly reproving way I remembered all his friends doing. I could tell she still missed him terribly.

The Burningbush golf club was rich with the smells of leather and burning logs, with quiet good cheer and mementos of a treasured past—crossed swords and tartans, enormous trophies and pictures of ancient captains staring down from the walls. The bartender, my one link with that day in 1956, fondly reminisced about his extraordinary friend. I learned then that Shivas had never actually worked for the golf club itself. He had been a teaching professional in his own employ; he had wanted it that way to "preserve his peculiar teaching ways."

"Oh, there was no one else like 'im, that's for sure," the barman said and smiled wistfully. " 'Cept for Seamus, and he's gone, too." Seamus MacDuff, whom Shivas called his teacher, had died a few years before. So had Julian Laing, the town's remarkable doctor, who was another of Shivas's special friends. Evan Tyree, the well-known golf champion and his most famous pupil, had gone to New Zealand in some mysterious land deal. And the McNaughton family had moved to Africa. All the people I had met fourteen years before had vanished, except for this good-natured rotund barman, red-faced and grayer than when I had seen him last.

I introduced myself, suddenly aware of how important he was, my last link with Shivas Irons conceivably.

"Liston's my name," he said, reaching out a hand, "just call me Liston. Christian name's Sonny, but the men here call me Liston." He slipped me a glass of Scotch—and then another—and we spent the afternoon reminiscing about our departed friend while he served the club members and kept the fire, which I remembered so well, burning brightly.

"It was amazin' to watch him come on to the people here," he said, "he was so different with each and every one, if ye watched him close. So I can see wha' ye mean when ye say he changed his shape. I watched him for so many years, watched him grow up, ye know. He was more fascinatin' the more ye watched him. My wife used to say she could tell when we'd been togither—said I picked up his way o' talkin' and gesturin'. Funny thing about that, she liked it when I'd been around 'im, said I seemed to like *her* more afterwards." He shook his head with the knowing smile of a husband who has been through the marital wars. "He was a vivid one awright. Ye know another peculiar thing? I've been thinkin' about 'im lately, been thinkin' o' the way he hit his practice shots out there," he pointed out a window to a deserted tee. "There was somethin' about the way he hit those shots tha' used to get to me—and still does—somethin' funny. I still think about that swing o' his . . . and the look on his face." I asked him if he and Shivas ever talked about the philosophical side of the game. "Very seldom," he said, "hardly ever, come to think of it. I never understood his talk about the inner mind and such, but he never talked much like tha', just now and then wi' someone like yersel', someone on to philosophical things. But with everyone he talked—never knew 'im to be lost for words. Course most o' the men here wanted his advice from time to time, and he was quick to give it."

I asked him if he had any idea about where Shivas might be. "No idea at all," he said. "Somethin' was gettin' to him though, toward the end. He talked a lot about the need to move on, heard him say that to the people here before he left. Sometimes too he talked about his needin' to help the poor." He shook his head as if he were puzzled. "And then there was quite a bit o' talk about his galavantin'. 'Twas said he had some problems wi' the women. 'Twas even said he was a little off when it came to the ladies." He pointed a finger at his head as he said this. "But of coorse 'twas said about him generally from time tae time—just a little off." Again the finger was pointed at the head. "But he was aye guid to me, and a great one for singin' and enjoyin'. No one else could sing a ballad like 'im."

After more conversation, it became apparent that Liston still missed his friend keenly, and was telling the truth when he said Shivas had left no traces. No one in Burningbush, it seemed, knew how I could find him.

I left Scotland in a heavy depression. I had waited so long

to see him again, a place in my consciousness had been prepared for our eventual meeting. The depression lasted until I decided to write this book. Writing it would summon his presence, I thought, and indeed it has. Digging into my memory for clues to his character and state of mind has yielded unexpected insights. Once I began to write, I realized that that one day in 1956 had enough in it to last me a lifetime, especially if I put some of his admonitions to work.

Having completed this book, I realize there was far more to Shivas Irons than I have been able to capture. Some of his enigmatic remarks, all those journals of his I never opened, and the unexplained events of that day in 1956 constantly remind me of that. There is much about our meeting that is still obscure. I have decided to put forth what I have, however, rather than wait for the day of final clarity, which may yet be a long way off.

And also—I must admit it—a hope lurks that this slender volume will lure its real author out of hiding.

A Footnote Regarding His Name

As I have said, "Burningbush" is a fanciful name for the actual golfing links in Fife upon which my adventures took place. The same is true for the names of three or four characters in the story. But I have left the name of my protagonist intact: Shivas Irons was the appellation he had carried all his life. It is so unusual that I have looked up its etymology; and indeed there are records of its origins and history. Shivas or Shives is a Scottish family name, which was known in East Aberdeenshire as early as the fourteenth century; a district there has sometimes been known as Shivas. *Chivas Regal* is a famous Scotch whisky. In Scots dialect there is a verb "shiv" or "shive," which means to push or shove; perhaps the family took its name from some early conquest in which it pushed the older peoples out. There is also a noun "shive," which means a slice of bread; I would prefer to think that his name derived from that, since he offered me the very bread of life in his presence and wisdom. There is also the noun "shivereens," which has approximately the same meaning as the word "smithereens," namely fragments, atoms, shivers ("he was blown to smithereens"); that relationship is apropos, seeing what he did to certain people's perceptions. I could find no connection though with the ancient Hindu name for the God of Destruction and Redemption, perhaps the oldest of all living words for Deity (icons of Shiva date back to the second or possibly the third millennium B.C.). That was a disappointment, but I have consoled myself by remembering that direct etymologies are not the only sign of inner connection.

The name "Irons" was known in the region of Angus as early as the fifteenth century. I have not been able to trace a clan connection for it, however (or for Shivas). Every bit of knowledge regarding his ancestry holds great fascination, I find, increasingly so as my hopes of seeing him again continue to fade, for perhaps the family history will give me some clue to his character. The Scots word "iron" (or "irne") is interesting in this regard, for it means a sword. That it came to mean a golf club suggests an important turn in the Scottish character. Indeed, it also came to mean a part of the plow. Turning swords to plowshares is, as I like to see it, one of the chief promises the game holds out for us.

Shivas Irons: it is such an appropriate name for the man. What did his parents have in mind when they laid it on him? Another Scottish philosopher, Thomas Carlyle, said a name surrounds us all our life like a cloak and ". . . what mystic influence does it not send inwards, even to the centre; especially in those plastic first-times, when the whole soul is yet infantine, soft, and the invisible seedgrain will grow to be an all overshadowing tree!" A name can shape a life, and if his soul took birth to do the work I found him doing, how well his parents sensed it and named him for the task.

Golf in the Kingdom

Personal charm is a physical thing. It also carries elements of endless surprise. Physical and surprising, matter and something new, bodying forth what you would never expect. From the very beginning that is what my encounter with Shivas Irons was like.

The pro shop at Burningbush stands behind the first tee, some 30 yards from the imposing clubhouse. The little building seemed familiar as I entered, for I had read about it in a book of memoirs by a famous Scots golf professional. There was even a sense of *déjà vu* as I looked around the place; I could have sworn I had seen the little man behind the starter's desk before. He showed me the clubs and shoes he had to rent, studying me, as he did, with a sly curiosity. I could tell he was watching as I waggled some of the woods and irons.

"Are ye lookin' for a game?" he asked. I said that I was. Having heard so much about the difficulties of Burningbush Links and its well-known obstacles, I felt I could use some support and guidance going around it.

"Are ye an American?" he asked as he fussed with his equipment display.

"Yes, I am," I replied.

"A toorist heer?"

"I'm a student. I've heard a lot about Burningbush and always wanted to play it. I had a dream once I played it."

"Wha' ye studyin'?"

"Philosophy. I'm on my way to India." I was a little embarrassed saying it. I usually was in those days, especially around men. Indian philosophy was neither practical nor completely manly.

He watched me put on a pair of golf shoes and choose the set of clubs I wanted.

"Well, I think I can get ye a game," he said after a moment's silence. "There's a professional here takin' someone for a teachin' round. Maybe ye'd like to play along wi' them?"

I was delighted. A pro could help me out there on Lucifer's Rug, I said, referring to one of the links' famous hazards.

"Oh, he may help ye now, and then again he may na'. There they are, out there." He pointed through the pro shop window to a pair of men talking on the first tee.

I gathered up the paraphernalia I had rented and carried it outside to a little bench, then took out the driver for some practice swings. The two figures were conversing about 30 feet away. They stood with their backs to me, looking down the first fairway. The taller of the two, obviously the teacher, was pointing to a distant object and explaining something with a voice that conveyed a strong sense of authority. I walked toward them and hesitantly cleared my throat to announce my arrival. They continued talking, apparently unaware that I was there. I cleared my throat again and ventured a small "Hello." The taller one, the teacher, turned to face me. That penetrating, disconcerting look—I realized at once that we had already met!

About an hour before, I had taken a wrong turn on my way to the clubhouse. By mistake I had gone down a path behind the caddies' shelter and had come to a dark, narrow corridor between the shelter and a high embankment. About 15 feet away from me, a figure was jumping grotesquely and kicking at an overhanging beam some 10 feet above the ground. With each kick the jumping figure would twist and fall back, breaking the fall with outstretched arms. The performance was repeated several times. He was apparently trying to kick the beam, trying to reach a point as high as a basketball hoop with his foot instead of his hand! Not knowing whether to intrude or retreat, I stood transfixed in the shadows of the passageway as this strange performance continued in silence. The only sound the jumper made was a weightlifter's explosive exhalation before each effort. He was totally unaware of my presence. After five or six arabesques in midair, he finally grazed the beam above him with the toe of his shoe—I realized it was a golf shoe!—and landed on his chest and stomach. For a moment he lay with his face to the ground, breathing deeply. Then he looked up and saw me staring down at him with embarrassed fascination.

He stood up without a word, pulling himself to his full height, some six feet two or three, and I met that uncanny look for the first time. It was ever so slightly cross-eyed—perhaps from the jumping—something wild and serene, for a second the space between us wavered.

Then, suddenly, he grinned and a second face appeared, an entirely different emanation, a look that was immensely warm and engaging with a big, slightly bucktoothed grin. He winked and wagged his head with an ironic gleam—as if to say, "Hang in there, boy"—and walked past me without a word. As he went past, I could smell him. It was the smell of eucalyptus and baking bread, a powerful and distinctive odor.

Now here we were face to face again. A shock of untamed reddish hair fell across his forehead and his blue unsettling eyes looked straight into mine. I introduced myself. He smiled his bucktoothed smile again and said in his resonant Scots dialect, "Shivas Irons ma nemme, and this gentleman is Mr. Balie MacIver." He pointed to his playing partner, then turned abruptly to look down the fairway. I brought my golf clubs up to the tee blocks and took a few practice swings, relieved that he was preoccupied with the lesson he was giving.

While I practiced swinging, I watched them. It was hard to follow their Scottish idiom, but I got an idea that he was giving MacIver a kind of game plan for the entire round. "Noo, we'll play six holes for the centered swing, six tae feel gravity, and six tae scoor," he said—or something to that effect. Then they stood for a moment with their eyes closed, as if they were praying. Maybe they were saying the Lord's Prayer, I thought, like professional football teams do before a game.

After their brief meditation they started taking their practice swings. MacIver took his with a long iron. "Nae. Use yer play club noo," said the professional, pointing to his pupil's driver. As I would learn eventually, he believed that "driving" was a term that by its very connotation threw some golfers off their truest swing. He preferred to say that he was "playing" the ball on a drive, and called a driver a "play club," as golfers had done in centuries past.

As I watched him I could see he was not your ordinary golf professional. His look was an important part of his teaching. To emphasize a point he would impale MacIver with it, then flash his big engaging smile when a point had been conveyed. As I moved closer I saw that his left eye was slightly off focus—not enough to be readily perceptible, but enough to be disconcerting. It was focused ever so slightly to the center, giving his steady blue eyes a penetrating quality, almost as if he were looking at you from two vantage points at once. "Murphy," he said turning to me, "ye swing at the grass real purty, hav' a try at the ball"—a challenging invitation. He smiled as he said it and gestured toward the tee.

As I teed up my ball I looked down the gently rolling fairway. It was serenely inviting in the afternoon sun, but I knew from my reading that hazards lurked along its course all the way to the green. I could hear the pounding of ocean waves beyond the rough and see them breaking over boulders within range of an errant drive. The anticipation of playing Burningbush and this unusual golf professional's commanding presence had thrown me off—I remember wishing we could stop to pray again. As I addressed the ball I knocked it off the tee with the club face. Shivas Irons seemed to be seven feet tall as I glanced back. He looked down at me with compassionate good humor, as if he were rooting me on. He made one small gesture, a brief movement of his hand in front of his hips, palm held downward. I instantly knew what he meant. As I teed the ball up again I settled into a feeling of stomach and hips, making a center there for my swing. And then a vivid image appeared in my mind's eye, of a turquoise ball traveling down the right side of the fairway with a tail hook toward the green. I took my stance and waggled the club carefully, aware that the image of the shot was incredibly vivid. Then I swung and the ball followed the path laid down in my mind.

"Guid shot," he said loudly, "ha' did ye ken tae hit it thair? 'Tis the best lie tae the green."

"Just luck," I mumbled and stood aside, relieved that I had gotten past the first obstacles so well.

MacIver swung with what seemed to be a mere half-effort and his drive traveled 180 yards or so down the middle of the fairway. "That's it, that's it," the professional's voice rumbled with its heavy brogue. MacIver was dressed in white shoes and pants and a black cardigan sweater. It was a striking costume, all the more so because he seemed so modest. He was completely devoted to his teacher's admonitions, listening carefully to every word of instruction, concentrating utterly upon the game. He mumbled something and quickly stepped aside, smiling proudly in spite of himself.

It was the professional's turn now. He stooped down gracefully to tee his ball, balancing for a moment on one leg as if to test his balance and spring. It was a kind of ritual dance he was to repeat on several holes. Then he stood addressing the ball for a few seconds, a brief address, but during that moment all his attention came to awesome focus. Like Ben Hogan, he seemed to peer into the very center of the ball and summon a secret strength. I could feel the energy gathering, feel it in my solar plexus, a powerful magnetic field drawing everything into itself—and then his swing unfurled, slower than I had anticipated after that awesome address but impacting with immense power and following through with utter grace and balance. I held my breath as the ball flew, stretching as if to hold it in the sky. It sailed 280 yards or more down the middle of the fairway—hovering there longer than any shot I had ever seen—then it landed, bouncing high toward the green. He picked up his tee, winked, and gave a little kick to suggest the performance I had watched behind the clubhouse. "Someday perhaps the ba' will na' come down again," he said with a smile. "Have ye e'er had tha' feelin'?" He was obviously pleased. It had been an awesome shot.

He walked ahead of us down the fairway with a long rhythmic stride, a russet sweater tapering from broad shoulders to a pair of hips as well formed and contoured as a football player's. He wore a pair of golden-brown corduroy pants and ordinary brown golf shoes. I found it hard to take my eyes off him. He stopped by MacIver's ball and watched his pupil make the next shot, another half-effort that landed in front of the green.

By now MacIver was totally preoccupied with his game. His swing was neither graceful nor powerful, but it was impressive to see his concentration and total devotion to the discipline his teacher had set for him. I felt a twinge of envy for their collusion.

I hit a seven iron onto the green—the example they were setting was having its effect. Shivas hit a wedge 3 feet from the cup, with the same grace and power he had shown with his drive. I was beginning to feel a sense of awe as I watched him, something I have always felt around consummate athletes. He birdied, I parred, MacIver bogeyed the hole. I wrote a four on my scorecard; MacIver was keeping score for them.

"Ah like yer swing, Michael," he said as we walked to the

second tee, giving me that sudden smile. The remark startled me. I was touched that he called me Michael, that he had noticed my shot.

"Any chance of getting a lesson?" I answered, blurting out the thought that was running through my mind.

He looked directly into my eyes. "Oh, but ye may na' ken tha' that is a solemn and serious matter, a serious matter indeed." He smiled good-naturedly, but I could see that he meant it. Then he grinned and reached out to shake my hand. "Just call me Shivas," he said.

"Do you teach here all summer?"

"It depends," he replied, then turned away without further explanation.

The second green could be seen from the tee, some 353 yards away according to the scorecard, down a straight, gently rolling fairway. The rough on the right was full of stones and gorse, or "whin" as it is sometimes called, the small spiny bush that grows on Scottish links-land. An incoming fairway ran down the left side. Not a very difficult hole, I said to myself as I surveyed it. MacIver hit another short, unpretentious shot down the middle, conscientiously following the game plan. It was my turn now. Once again an image came of the ball in flight—a turquoise ball down the middle —and so it flew. I had somehow developed the knack of seeing the shot in my mind's eye as I addressed the ball. On both drives it had appeared spontaneously, a bright, compelling image. Was I learning something just being around them? Shivas was next. Again the ritual dance as he teed the ball, and again the awesomely concentrated address. He split the fairway with a lower drive this time, something more like a rifle shot. As I was to learn later, he never used the same swing twice—or so he said—though it was difficult for me to see the changes.

As we walked up the fairway, I took the scorecard out and looked at the yardage figures. The course was about 6800 yards long, not too long to play in par. To shoot a par round at Burningbush, that would be something to remember! I began calculating how many birdies I would need, maybe two or three on the par fives, maybe one or two more on the other holes, that would give me a chance for a 72 or better with the bogies I was bound to make. I hurried my steps to see what kind of lie I had for my second shot. The ball was near the center of the fairway, about an eight-iron shot from the green. Maybe I could get a birdie on this one, I thought. Then images of veering shots started to form in my mind. Images of the gorse, of the bunkers in front of the green, of the rocks behind it. I began adjusting my swing as I addressed the ball. The poise I had felt on the drive had disappeared; excitement, anticipation, and bobbing images of disaster had taken its place. I backed away, and approached the ball again—and then as I began to swing, a picture came of the gorse to the right. I pulled the shot to the left, into the adjoining fairway. I slammed the club into the bag and hurried toward my ball, not waiting for the others.

"Now, hold there, Michael," Shivas's authoritative voice came booming across the fairway. "Just wait yer toorn." He was suddenly stern as he looked at me.

I stopped in mid-stride and waited for them to play. As I stood watching Shivas make his shot—another lovely approach onto the green—my fantasies of an exceptional score continued. I pulled out the scorecard again to see which holes were par fives.

When I got to the ball, I saw that a bunker stood between it and the green. The pin was about 100 feet away, just a pitch and run for a par. I pulled a nine iron from my bag and took a few practice swings, adjusting them for distance and roll. With each practice swing the bunker got larger. I backed away twice from the ball—but to no avail. As I swung, I looked up and the ball landed in the sand. I lifted back my head and stared up at the sky, hovering somewhere between a curse and a prayer. Shivas and MacIver watched in silence. As I disappeared into the bunker they waved and shouted some words of encouragement, but that was the only sound until I blasted onto the green and two-putted for a double bogey. My fantasies of a 72 at Burningbush had been dealt a blow.

A little bench stood behind the third tee. MacIver sat down on it and began writing scores on his card. To my surprise he wanted to know what I had shot on the two holes we had played. "I'll keep my own score," I said. "You have your lesson. Don't bother." I didn't want to say it out loud, that I had shot a six. We all knew, but saying it out loud was harder. But MacIver insisted that he keep all our scores. "Four on the first, and a six on the second," I finally said. "That damn bunker, and I should have sunk the putt. . . ."

"Ye had a five oon the first," Shivas interrupted me sternly.

I turned to face him. He was looking straight at me, with that steady cross-eyed gaze. "Ye must count that one ye knocked off the tee when ye took yer waggle," he said solemnly.

Have you ever felt as you talked to someone that everything was turning unreal? That is exactly how I felt then, as I realized what he was saying. The shock of this all-seeing scrutiny, the small-mindedness of it, and the embarrassment I felt for violating their code of honor drew the blood to my stomach.

"So, a five and a six?" MacIver asked.

Shivas could see I was having a hard time answering. "Now, Michael," he said, raising a long finger and shaking it at me, "ye must rimember that ye're in the land where all these rools were invented. 'Tis the only way ye can play in the kingdom." Then the big grin appeared, his second face. I can't remember what I said in reply, but I submitted to the discipline.

I have thought of that line many times, "the only way you can play in the kingdom." I didn't fully appreciate it at first. Not until I realized that for him the Kingdom of Fife was very nearly the Kingdom of Heaven.

But I was not ready to appreciate it then. Even though he

had reached out to me, I could feel his scrutiny. I felt a growing edge of resentment as we got ready for our drives—it was going to be hard to shoot a 72.

But my hopes did not die easily. The upcoming hole was a par five, a possible birdie—I could get a stroke back there, one or two more on the other par fives, shoot even on the rest, and still get a 72. I made my own game plan as I watched MacIver get ready to drive. Go all out on the drive, I thought, but keep it smooth—I formed an image of Snead's strong, rhythmic backswing and combined it with a picture of Shivas's concentration as he stood up to the ball. Or just swing like Shivas himself; that is what I resolved to do as I teed up and took my stance. I waggled the club carefully, remembering the first tee, picturing Shivas as he took his stance, thinking also of Snead as I had seen him once during a driving contest at Pebble Beach. I peered fiercely into the ball and swung. It sailed in a long sweeping hook, an impressive sailing carry across fairway and rough, far out into the gorse. It was perhaps the longest shot I had ever hit.

I began to grit my teeth as if I were biting some invisible opponent. Exhilaration over this sudden power was mixed with the utter frustration of my deteriorating score. I asked Shivas if I could hit another in case the ball was lost.

"No, not heer," he said forbiddingly, "ye can aye find it in tha' particular ruif."

Again there was a sense of unreality about our exchange. As he got ready to shoot I slammed my club into the bag and swore out loud. It didn't seem to faze him though; he hit another amazing drive down the middle of the fairway.

The rough along the third hole at Burningbush is full of rocks and gorse. Gorse, a low brambly shrub of the genus *Ulex*, is common to Scottish wastelands and golfing links. It is said by some to grow as well in the fields of Hell. Occasionally, a ball will come to rest upon its top branches a foot or two above the ground. In that case one is required to play out, since the shot is possible—barely. That was my good fortune then. I could see my ball as I approached, nestling on its thorny cushion awaiting deliverance.

In playing a shot like this you must be careful not to jostle the bush in any way, for the ball may sink deeper into its branches. Knowing this, I carried my bag of clubs in a wide arc around the ball and stepped toward it slowly, seven iron in hand, determined to hit my approach within range of the green. An image of par still danced in my head, in spite of all the omens. I held the iron away from the yellow blossoms as I took my stance, as one does in a sand trap, and lined up my feet. I started the club back a few times to see that my swing would not be impeded by rocks or gorse—there was plenty of room. I eyed the flag, still so far way. Then as I began to swing in earnest, the ball sank gently out of sight among the flowers on that innocent bush. I looked up to the sky and shook my head. "This fucking game," I said, "this fucking game."

"How does it lie?" Shivas's stentorian voice suddenly reverberated across the gorse. He stood watching me from the edge of the fairway some thirty yards away.

"It fell into the middle of a whin," I yelled back. "Should I play it, or drop out?" Perhaps he would show me some mercy.

"No, play it like it lies," he yelled. "It'll come out."

I cursed him silently. Since the ball was invisible now I had to guess how deep my seven iron should cut into the shrub. I lined up again, eyeing the distant flag, testing my backswing for potential obstacles. Then I chopped down viciously. Yellow flowers flew in all directions, a veritable shower of gold, but no ball was forthcoming.

"Bring me a bouquet when ye come oot," he bellowed. I looked at him standing there. I couldn't believe it, it must have been the Scottish sense of humor.

"I can't even see the ball," I shouted back. "I think I should drop out."

"It'll come out," he answered. "Keep choppin'."

I swung again, even harder than I had the first time, and hit a rock as I hit the ball. Sparks flew in all directions, a second shower of gold. The ball flew about 30 feet, into another patch of gorse.

"Fucking bastard," I said, chopping furiously at the devastated bush. "Fuck the score." Shivas had turned away and was walking toward his ball. I felt an urge to give him the finger.

I hit a wedge shot onto the fairway and joined MacIver. I was lying four and hadn't even reached his modest drive yet.

At about this point I began to feel like revenge—against Shivas, the course, even MacIver for his plodding game. I would hit a 250-yard three wood onto the green and hole the putt for a bogey, a prodigious recovery; that would show them. I thought of Snead again as I lined up, of Hogan, Jimmy Thompson, George Bayer, a whole array of potent images to summon my strength. I threw everything into the shot—and topped it badly. It bounced straight up and landed about 20 or 30 feet away. Poor MacIver, he was trying to give me room, trying not to interfere with my struggle while concentrating in his own methodical way. Still he could not suppress the urge to give me some advice. He was a middle-aged, kindly-looking man, with a trim mustache and crisp manners, perhaps an Army officer judging from his bearing. "Now, Murphy," he said, "just try usin' yer short irons tae finish the hole." It was the most galling remark of all.

I mumbled something in reply, and watched him hit another inexorable shot down the middle.

Shivas was standing near his ball, ahead of us to our right.

"The twa o' ye remind me o' the tortoise and the hare," he said. I gritted my teeth and shook my head to acknowledge the fact that I had heard him.

My ball now had large gashes in it, and when I hit my next shot—with a five iron, dejectedly following MacIver's advice —it wobbled in flight as a ball will do after being so badly treated. It veered in two directions like a wounded bird.

"Guid man!" cried our professional. " 'Tis the first time Ah e'er saw a hook and a slice on one shot." I was beginning to think I was his straight man.

He put his three wood on the green, hitting the very shot I had visualized for myself.

When we got to the green Shivas lay two and was putting for an eagle; MacIver lay four, just 3 feet from the pin; and I lay seven. I was tempted to pick up, but sensed what they would say. In spite of my growing resentment, Shivas's authoritative presence was enough to keep me quiet. I marked my ball and started to clean it. The gashes I had given it smiled hideously, it would be impossible to putt. "May I put down another ball?" I asked meekly. Neither of them answered. Perhaps they were too sorry for me to say no. But they were not sorry enough to say yes. I put the mutilated ball back on the putting surface. As I bent down to make the putt I had the impression—I can remember it to this day— that one of the gashes winked at me. It's only a game after all, it seemed to say, only a game. When I putted, the point was made more vividly. The ball veered to the left like one of those trick balls that are sold for practical jokes. The thought occurred that I would never get it into the hole.

MacIver sunk his putt for a par, his first of the round. Shivas narrowly missed his, ending up with another birdie. I tried again. This time the ball veered to the right, stopping about 3 feet from the cup. Then Shivas, who had been looking away during the entire performance, turned and said, "Noo try willin' it in, it'll never get there in the regular coorse o' things." He meant to be helpful, I suppose. I glowered back at him, my first act of overt defiance. I hit the putt without lining it up, not caring where it went. It rolled straight at last, hit the back of the cup, bounced high and came to rest on the other side. Seeing it lying there, I remembered something I had seen my brother Dennis do back in our high school days. Following his example, I leaned back and looked at the sky, then raised my arm to God and gave Him the finger. My two playing partners laughed and turned away. I tapped the ball into the hole and we walked off the green in silence.

On the next tee, MacIver, methodical again after my display, took out his score card and wrote down their scores. "How many, Murphy?" he asked crisply, peering at the card. I stared at him for a moment. He peered at the scorecard, waiting for my reply. How many! They were going to count them! "Just give me an X," I said.

"A what?" He looked at me as if he did not comprehend.

"I'm not counting that hole," I said.

"Noo, Michael," said Shivas, "put doon yer score, it'll do ye good."

I could tell he was trying to reassure me, but I also sensed their incredible sense of honor about keeping score. My dropping out offended their whole sense of things.

"An X?" asked MacIver, as if he hadn't heard me right.

"Oh, put down a ten," I finally said with exasperation.

For a moment there was silence. MacIver stared at the scorecard, pursing his lips, somehow reluctant to write it down. Shivas cocked his head to one side as if he were thinking. It was a silence full of unspoken thoughts. Finally, MacIver lifted a hand to scratch his ear and looked at his teacher for advice. Shivas looked solemnly at me.

"Michael, Ah think 'twas eliven," he said.

MacIver looked at me, waiting for my assent. "An eleven," I said, nodding with resignation, and he carefully wrote it down.

Shivas came over to me then and put a big hand on my shoulder. "Dona' worry aboot the score so much," he said, "it's not the important thing." He squeezed my shoulder and turned back to MacIver with more instructions. Not the important thing, I thought as he walked away, not the important thing! I was touched by his reaching out—and dumfounded.

Scoring not the important thing! While they watched me like hawks! I thought about it all the way to the fourth tee.

When frustration grew to the breaking point during a round of golf I would do either one of two things—get ostentatiously slaphappy and hit my shots in any direction as if it were the outing that was important, or play with concentrated fury. I went into the latter mode on hole number four—I would show them. Playing that way, I would think of Ben Hogan, his Indian profile cutting through every obstacle, and squint my eyes like a prairie scout. I would begin an interior conversation, or rather a stream of incantations that had as their goal the willing of the ball to its target. It was a kind of black magic, whereby the mind forced itself upon the ball and steered it right in spite of all the errors my body committed. I sometimes tried it at baseball and football games. I had even developed a whammy which, when used properly, could bring a man down.

I gathered myself for the attack as we got ready to tee off. I summoned images of fierce swingers like Hogan and Bayer, with something of Shivas's own concentration thrown in, and glowered down the fairway. When I stood up to the ball I held my stance for a long time, eyes squinting, showing them that I really meant business now, and imagined the ball rocketing toward the green. I hit an exceptionally long drive.

It was a 400-yard par four, curving to the left. The drive cut across the corner of the dog-leg, leaving me a seven iron to the green. I hit my second with the same concentrated anger, a low shot that sailed true—and sailed over the green into some unknown hazard. I had willed it with all my might, and had willed it too well: I had hit the shot some 20 yards farther than I ordinarily did with a seven iron from that kind of lie.

We never found the ball. It had disappeared into a rocky draw that led down to the ocean. Perhaps it had bounced into the waves. So I dropped a second ball and shot a double bogey.

·When we finished the hole, I sat on a rock and looked at the waves. Shivas came over and laid a hand on my shoulder I suppose he could tell I was losing heart. "Ye try too hard and ye think too much," he said with the authority that Scots golf professionals often assume. "Why don't ye go wi' yer pretty swing? Let the nothingness into yer shots." His words made me feel better. It did seem silly to ruin all the beautiful scenery with the fuss I was making.

The next hole was a kind of purgatory after the hell I had put myself through. Perhaps it was the influence of his advice and its apparent success with MacIver, perhaps it was the resignation I felt about my score. In any case I managed to get a bogey five, playing each shot as carefully as MacIver had been doing. The tortoise was teaching the hare.

I had overheard Shivas telling his pupil to think of the ball and "sweet spot" belonging together. The "sweet spot" is the place on the clubface where the ball should be struck; one might hit a decent shot, even a very good one, and not hit it exactly, but when you do there is no mistaking it—to hit it is the very essence of golfing pleasure. Shivas had told MacIver that the ball and the sweet spot were "already joined." "Just see it that way," he had said, "they're aye joined afore ye started playin'." The advice helped. I began to imagine them fitting together as I laid the clubhead behind the ball. It helped settle me down. I had—almost in spite of myself— joined MacIver to form a small procession following in our teacher's impressive wake.

For the next few holes our game was relatively uneventful. MacIver continued keeping my score—he was probably incapable of doing otherwise—and I continued thinking that the clubface and the ball were one. I watched Shivas whenever I could, and slowly his example began to influence me in a peculiar way. I became more and more aware of the *feeling* of the game, of how it was to walk from shot to shot, how it was to feel the energy gathering as I addressed the ball, how the golf links smelled. It was not that he said anything to me, but his example. He was so physical in the way he moved and responded, like a big animal. The only thing he asked me in fact during those middle holes was whether I could smell the heather. "It's growin' way over there," he said, pointing to a distant hill, "but ye can smell it from heer." I could smell it, and though I didn't tell him, I could also smell that powerful odor of eucalyptus and baking bread.

Those middle holes were a lesson in resignation and simple sensing. No more ambitions for prodigious shots and scores, they seemed out of reach; just a decent modest game and enjoyment of the endless charms of Burningbush. It was a new way to play for me; I had always been so focused on the score and the mechanics of my swing. I had always tried for spectacular shots—long drives, approaches stiff to the pin, shots I could talk about and collect like medals in my golfing memory. Now my focus of awareness included other things, like the heather and the waves coming in from the sea.

The holes ran along water, and you could see for miles along the sandy links land, across gently rolling hillocks lavender and yellow in the afternoon sun. Better sights to fill my memory with than mutilated golf balls and careening shots.

MacIver now had gone into the second phase of his game plan. He was working on something called "true gravity"— something, as far as I could make out, that involved an awareness of "energy-dimensions" and the relations of things. Following Shivas's instruction, he was trying to "see" the subtle fields of energy that were supposed to surround the ball, the club, and his very own body. Although they kept me out of their conversations, I overheard them discussing it from time to time and began to see if I could understand what it was all about. I had heard other strange theories during my golfing travels—golfers keep coming up with amazing things along this line—but nothing quite so organized as this. MacIver was now trying to see the one energy field that enveloped his body, ball, and club. For the first holes he had been focusing exclusively on the ball and clubface, he was extending it now to include the rest.

I tried it for three or four shots but nothing seemed to happen. I did keep my eye on the ball, however, and that was a gain. Maybe that is what these things are all about, I thought, ways to keep a person looking at the ball—anything to help concentration. Plenty of other things had been tried, God knows, why not metaphysics? Though I failed to see the auras MacIver was looking for I felt a new elasticity in my swing. Then on the ninth hole I did see something. It wasn't much, just the tiniest glimpse, but I did seem to see a yellow light around a sea gull swooping in from the sea. Then as I was driving on the tenth it happened again, a tiny aura around the ball, a violet one this time. When I hit the ball I hit the sweet spot.

"That's the sound we want," said Shivas, as if he had been waiting to hear it. The drive was not particularly impressive, but it felt good.

As I walked toward the ball, I wondered if seeing those auras could be tricks of the retina. I told him what had happened and stated my doubts.

"Noo, Michael," he said firmly, "when ye think tha' maybe it's yer retina, ye'r just one step awa' from really seein' things." On my approach shot I hit the sweet spot again, after watching the "aura" expand and contract, and the ball landed 20 feet from the pin. I told him what had happened after we finished the hole. "Keep swingin'," he said. Just the two words, nothing more.

I parred ten and eleven, fascinated with what I would see and feel on each shot. This was a new kind of game for me, a series of strange sensations and intuitions, my first exposure to that order of things called "true gravity." But I could only sustain it for a while. On the twelfth hole our drive was into the wind, down a narrow fairway that dog-legged to the right. Familiar images of disaster came back to haunt me as I took my stance. I sliced the drive and the sea breeze carried it into the rough. Shivas walked along beside me up the fairway, and asked me what I was thinking. I told him about the awful thoughts. "They'll pass," he said, "if ye daena' fight 'em. Come back to where'er ye were a minute ago. Wait 'em oot." Those words were a great help—not only for the rest of the round but for my life ever since. The admonition to "wait

'em oot" was one of those sayings of his that came back
to haunt me.

I managed the hole in bogey, by hitting a conservative
wedge from the rough and approaching the green with a five
iron. When MacIver asked my score there was pleasure in
saying that I had made a five—such a different reaction from
the one I had felt on the third tee! Even a bogey seemed
good, everything was beginning to carry some unexpected
satisfaction.

We had now come to the thirteenth hole, which is famous
in golfing circles. It is a par three up a hill, to a pin that
stands silhouetted between a pair of twisted cypress trees.
Between the tee and the green lies Lucifer's Rug, a field of
clotted gorse, 200 yards of it to catch any shot that is
less than perfection. Along the left runs a steep ravine, from
which several boulders rise. It was fortunate, I thought as I
looked to the pin, that I had come to this concentrated state
of mind by now. Every Monday the caddies of Burningbush
and other links came here to hunt for lost golf balls, some
trained their dogs for the task. At various points in the history
of the club there had been efforts by members to have the
hole enshrined as a golf museum, thus prohibiting further
play upon it. It was even said that a body had once been
found "under the rug."

The tee shot had to carry to the green but not roll down
the other side, for another ravine dropped off there. Few
players could reach it with an iron, so in effect a wood was
required to do the work of a pitching wedge. To make matters worse, there was usually a wind across the rise—
witness the twisted cypress trees—so the shot had to be
played to the left, to the ravine side. It was a hole in all
respects suited to test the powers of "true gravity."

The wind was now blowing from left to right, hard enough
to lift the distant flag. I took out a two iron and gazed at its
sweet spot, as if it were an icon. MacIver seemed to be in a
trance as he stared dumbly up the hill. But Shivas went into
the oddest ritual of all. First he stood on his left leg, then on

his right, once with eyes open, once with them closed. Then he cupped his hands to his mouth and gave an incredible cry toward the ravine. It was a long wavering wail, something between a yodel and a cry for the departed dead. It sent a shiver up my back. We could hear its echo from the ravine, bouncing off the rocks. Then he turned and nodded gravely, indicating that we should proceed.

MacIver, apparently unfazed by this unexpected performance, took his driver and stood like a statue before his ball, a figure of total dedication. All dressed in white and black, he contrasted vividly with the ascending vista of yellow gorse. A tiny figure there, I had an image of him flying like Chagall in the wake of his shot. He stood motionless for a very long time, plumbing the depths of "true gravity," I suppose, and then he swung. It sailed straight and high—and landed in the gorse some 20 feet short of the summit. He grimaced as he turned toward his golf bag. I slowly marched to the firing line, praying to my golf club icon and looking intently for that mystical joining with the ball. I teed up. As I did there was another bloodcurdling cry, Shivas was wailing again behind my back. I was so startled I jumped. He shook his head apologetically, but said nothing—his attention seemed to be focused somewhere else.

Whether from the many holes of high concentration or from this incredible performance my mind seemed blasted empty. It was impossible to summon any image. I swung without thinking and the ball flew like a bullet on a low trajectory, a white streak against yellow, rising into the sky before it fell to the green. The picture of it is still painted brightly in my memory.

Shivas was smiling at me as I turned around. He winked as he went past, but his glance was wilder and more unsettling than ever. I walked over to my golf bag and slipped the iron into it, thinking as I did that maybe I should always pray to the club I was using. I was beginning to feel an exaltation about this round of golf. Then I turned to watch him make his shot. For a fleeting moment there was an odd distortion:

he seemed blurred as he stood there. To this day I do not know whether there were tears in my eyes from the wind or whether there was something else that caused it. He seemed smaller. And when he swung I could not see the ball in flight. I blinked as I looked up the hill, but it had disappeared. I asked MacIver as we walked to the green if he had seen it. He nodded vaguely; I could tell from his manner, though, that something odd had happened to him as well. That distortion seemed strange, however, only upon reflection later that day. The growing exaltation I was feeling possessed me then, crowded out questions, problems, anything that seemed not to fit. I felt the land as we climbed the hill, the sea breeze, the grass beneath my feet. A film had dropped from my eyes, from my hearing, from all my senses. The smell of the sea and the grass, of leather and perspiration filled the air. I could hear a cry of delight in the distance, then tiny cheers. Something had broken loose inside me, something large and free.

We found MacIver's ball and watched him play a little wedge shot to the green. And there upon the smooth green summit lay Shivas's ball and mine, just a foot apart near the pin. We played out in silence, a pair of birdies to go with MacIver's bogey, Shivas solemn and centered, not giving a hint of what was going through his mind.

I looked out from our vantage point; we could see for miles now. The sun was dipping behind the western hills, while purple shadows spread across the water and arabesques of grass below. The curving fairways and tiny sounds arising from them, the fields of heather, the distant seacaps were all inside my skin. A presence was brooding through it all, one presence interfusing the ball, the green, MacIver, Shivas, everything.

I played the remaining holes in this state of grace. Specters of former attitudes passed through me, familiar curses and excuses, memories of old shots, all the flotsam and jetsam of my golfing unconscious—but a quiet field of energy held me and washed them away. I can think of no better way to say it—those final holes played me.

There were moments when the thought occurred, "maybe this will disappear." The new-found strength, that too was questioned. But there was another thought, "wait 'em out," and eventually I did.

The incoming holes of Burningbush unfolded before us, wild and gentle by turns. I could see why they were so loved and famous. They are so much more than you can see at first, fierce as Lucifer's Rug and familiar as the old town that beckons from the surrounding hills. From the thunders of the North Sea to the gray stone houses and cobblestone streets, Burningbush shimmers in my memory.

As if to show us that virtue will be rewarded, the occult Powers and Dominions gave us a grand finale. Shivas hit a drive on the eighteenth hole that carried all the way home— to the green 320 yards away. He was hitting with a wind to his back, and he took it to full advantage, sailing the ball toward the ancient clubhouse with a fade along the fairway to the green. I hit a wedge to the pin for a birdie, following MacIver, who had done the same. One eagle and two birdies closed out the round.

Shivas put an arm around my shoulder. "Ye deseruv' a drink," he said, "come j'in me and ma friends." So we headed for the clubhouse bar. MacIver said good-by, dutifully setting a time for his next lesson. Before he left he announced our scores, so faithfully recorded, a 67 for his teacher, an 84 for him, and an 86 for me. "And, Murphy," he said with an admiration that surprised me, "ye shot a 34 comin' in, the same as Mr. Irons, which only proves"—he raised a finger for emphasis—"that true gravity works on this plane too." I shook his hand and followed Shivas into the famous Burningbush clubhouse.

Singing the Praises of Golf

Liston the barman was lighting a fire in the clubhouse bar as we entered. A few moments later I was sitting in front of the blazing logs, whisky glass in hand, listening to Shivas and his friends sing Scottish golfing songs. The fire in front of me and the subtle fire of Shivas's presence were warming me inside and out. I listened to them singing in their rich Fife accents,

> ". . . among the heather and the gorse,
> ye must remember of course,
> not tae lose yer balls at ol' Sin Tondress. . . ."

listened to their laughter and raillery, to the sounds of golfers stomping grass from their cleats, then a cheer from the eighteenth green—sounds that reminded me of a special Christmas when I was a child. I was filled with gratitude, my eyes filled with tears as I looked around that glowing room. The mood that had come over me out on the course, that sense of an enormous presence suffusing the world, was with me still. I could feel the wild and mysterious terrain of the Burningbush Links, those immense worlds waiting, but this warm place was at the center of my feelings now, the convivial faces and friendly words, the songs, the walls covered with dancing firelight. I felt as if I had found my way home at last.

For more than an hour I watched the clubmembers come and go, and gazed into the fire as I savored that incredible round. Shivas was greeting friends at the bar. I could hear his voice above the rest from time to time, giving encouragement or answering a friendly gibe; his presence seemed as important to them as it was to me.

During that hour no problems existed. But then questions began to form, began intruding themselves as they inevitably do. The aura of utter well-being was fading, and I began the return to my ordinary state of mind.

What was this strangely impressive man really up to? What was he doing on the thirteenth tee? There had been something uncanny about that hole, something I could not quite bring into consciousness. What had the bartender meant when he taunted him about "defiling the old men of Burningbush"? Later that evening some of these questions would be answered and others would be compounded.

He had invited me to dinner, interrupting my ruminations with a sudden shout from the bar. "Michael, ma good lad," he said, coming over and putting his hand on my shoulder, " 'tis time ye're exposed to the true complexities o' the gemme." I would soon find that the thoughts which had begun to disturb me were being developed at length by others.

The meal was to be at the home of the McNaughtons', he said as we left the clubhouse. I was surprised and flattered at the sudden invitation, and sensed his excitement about the gathering that was soon to take place. He had changed into a white crew-necked sweater, and either because of the clothes or a change of mood had a different look about him. He seemed less massive and concentrated, even a little smaller in size. His wind-burned face contrasted sharply with the sweater's whiteness, making him more handsome than ever. He hummed a tune as we walked along, some old Scotch ballad, I think, with a vaguely Oriental air, that mysterious longing and joy you catch sometimes in the wailing of the pipes.

The strange melody trailed off as we approached our destination; he seemed to be distracted. When we arrived at the McNaughtons' house, he touched my shoulder vaguely and murmured something about needing to be alone for a moment. "Ye go ahaid, Michael, they'll understand," he almost whispered the words, then wandered off down the street. Startled and embarrased, I explained to the handsome woman who answered the door that Shivas Irons had invited me to dinner and that now he had gone off down the street. She asked me to come in. As I stepped through the doorway, I looked back and saw him sitting on a window ledge looking up into the evening sky. He seemed to be lost in thought.

"Did ye play gowf with him today?" the handsome lady asked as she ushered me in. "He sometimes brings his playin' partners here afterwards." She introduced herself as Agatha McNaughton. Following her up the narrow staircase, I couldn't help noticing what a great figure she had—she moved ahead of me up the steep passageway with slow pleasurable steps.

The other guests had arrived and were sitting with their drinks around a stone hearth that framed an inviting fire. Above the mantel an ancient-looking pair of crossed swords gleamed in the firelight. The men stood to greet me. Peter McNaughton, Agatha's husband, was a vigorous-looking red-faced man in his fifties, perhaps twenty years Agatha's senior. He shook my hand, pulling me toward him with two muscular jerks. "Welcome to our guid café," he said with gusto. "What did ye do with our unpredictable friend?"

"He went for a walk. . . ."

"Waitin' for the moon to rise perhaps," he said and smiled, cutting me off in midsentence as if to save me embarrassment. "He may stay out thair for an hour or more. But here . . ." he introduced me around to the others—an imposing craggy-faced old Scotsman named Julian Laing, an English couple named Greene, and Peter's sixteen-year-old son, Kelly. Laing, it was explained to me, was the town's "main doctor"; he had delivered five thousand of the town's ten thousand inhabitants. He was also, I was to discover, a psychiatrist of sorts with remarkable, highly eccentric theories. As he shook my hand he winked enigmatically and asked if Shivas had brought me "through the eye of the needle." I wasn't exactly sure what he meant.

The Greenes were visiting from Cornwall, up to study the ecology of the Firth of Forth and tell Shivas their new theories about golfing links. Spirited, bouncy little people not much taller than five feet, they reminded me of a pair of elves from Tolkien's trilogy. His name was Adam and hers was Eve, they were meant for each other, they said. Everyone laughed at the familiar joke, which must have been trotted out for the hundredth time. Adam Greene taught "cosmic ecology" at a London "Free University." God knows how he supported himself. I think he had been an engineer or inventor before his turn to philosophy.

Peter McNaughton acted as master of ceremonies with enormous zest and a sense that this was a special gathering indeed. It was obvious that he was very proud of his friends. His son, Kelly, was over six feet tall, had a sardonic whisky brogue, and blushed whenever he smiled. He smiled when he shook my hand.

"Did ye git the traitment today?" he asked. The remark carried all sorts of insinuations. I mumbled something like "Yes, I did have quite a round, how did you know?" evoking a laugh from everyone.

"How do we know!" exclaimed Agatha, with a warm, richly textured brogue. "Why, that bad man wouldna' just let ye play an ordinary round of golf!" I felt like I'd been taken into the clan.

We sat around the fire drinking whisky and trading pleasantries. I couldn't stop thinking about Shivas down there on that window ledge, but no one else seemed concerned. There was excitement underlying the hospitable remarks, a sense of anticipation about this gathering. "And what do ye do to keep the body alive, Mr. Murphy?" Agatha asked. She wore a light brown woolen blouse that showed the contour of her breasts. I said something about being a student and aspiring writer. They wanted to know what school I went to and I told them. Old Laing then got the conversation going in earnest.

"Well, Murphy," he intoned with his gnarled burr, "as an aspiring man of words, will ye tell me whether words have a future? They've had a dismal past." He raised his brambly eyebrows and peered over his glass at me. He then looked around at everyone else and came on with another conversation opener. "Wuidna' all of ye agree tha' all logic, all human history, all our experience compel us to recognize tha' the only thing in life worth doin' is the will of God?" I hadn't expected that kind of statement. I thought of some people in my home town, Salinas, from the First Church of God of Prophecy.

No one seemed disposed to reply. Any further remarks would have to carry some metaphysical force. There was a long silence as we drank our Scotch and looked into the fire.

"Well, Shivas would agree with ye," Kelly said at last with his sardonic inflection.

"Aye, we've discussed the matter for years," the old doctor replied, "but ye ken how he is. Tomorra' he'll be tellin' Murphy heer that believin' in God is dangerous. He's the dangerous one, o' course." He repeated the words with affectionate irony, "He's the dangerous one." There was affection in the old man's voice as he invoked his friend's presence, but with it there was an unmistakable sense that Shivas Irons was indeed dangerous.

"As long as we're talking about him, shouldn't we tell him it's time to eat?" Eve Greene broke in. The McNaughtons replied, almost in unison, that there was no use disturbing him now, that he would come in good time. "Ye know how he is," they said protectively, and ushered us into their dining room. It was a long, low candlelit room with latticed windows and wood beams across the ceiling. The dining table was some 20 feet long, and 4 feet wide, a table for a banquet. Seated around it we seemed yards apart.

The McNaughtons' hospitality, the happy anticipation I

felt among this group of friends, the whisky, and the winds of Burningbush had all had their effect upon me. I was warmed and lifted high. Peering down the table at those faces in the candlelight I began to smile. It must have been an idiot smile. "Ye look so happy, Michael," Agatha said, "a round of golf with Shivas will do tha' to ye."

"Oh, where is he, where *is* he?" Eve Greene persisted, looking hopefully about the room over her attractive upturned nose. Her head barely made it over the edge of the table. Both she and Adam needed cushions to reach their dinner. "We've been looking forward to seeing him for weeks. Our theories about golf and evolution are growing larger every day."

"Aye, ma guid Greenes, yer theories were enormous awready," said Peter, lifting his glass high. "Let us drink a toast to all theories round, let us sing the praises of gowf." His always ruddy face was red with pleasure. "To gowf!" he exclaimed, and we all raised our glasses—of water, milk, or whisky, a makeshift but inspired toast to golf and the good life.

Agatha then brought in a large tureen of broth, full of dumplings. For a moment we ate in silence, savoring the aroma of that ancient Scottish potion. It smelled to me like heather and the breeze above the thirteenth hole, warmed with bullion and flour dumplings.

Suddenly, there was a loud knocking at the front door and Shivas's stentorian voice shouting, "Open up in the name o' the law." Peter hurried down the stairs and we could hear them talking below. Then Shivas appeared at the dining-room door. He was flushed and radiant.

"I, ma guid cronies, Ah see ye've waited for me. Is thair anything *at a'* left to eat?" He embraced Agatha with a bone-crunching hug and held her for a moment while she tried to squirm away. "Adam and Eve, love birds still," he grasped their hands, "what new theories have ye now? Julian Laing, protector o' Burningbush and ma very own soul!" He went round the table as he greeted everyone. "And *you.*" He squeezed the back of Kelly's neck and the tall boy punched him playfully in the stomach. "What d'ye think o' this group, Michael? A motley lot, wouldn't ye say?"

He was strikingly handsome, tanned and ruddy in his white sweater and golden pants. Something had given his spirits a tremendous lift.

"I see that I've gotten here at the right moment. Lay on, Mrs. McNaughton," he said in his booming voice. And we all began eating the impressive meal that Agatha laid in front of us. What a wife she was, I thought, lucky Peter. Shivas obviously appreciated her too. "Agatha, Agatha, ye remind me o' what I'm missin'," he said as he demolished a plate of stew.

It was somewhere between the stew and the dessert that Peter took charge of the conversation. "It was time," he said, "for each of us to account for golf's strange and lasting attraction." Since the Greenes were here with their new theories and as this was a gathering that was not likely to recur for a while, if ever, he said, we should each in turn tell what the endlessly mysterious sport was really about. The Greenes were by now virtually standing on their chairs, which seemed so much lower than the rest, to talk about their discoveries. They had been waiting for weeks for the occasion. Shivas was enthusiastic too. " 'Tis time tha' we did justice to the subject," he said, "and this is just the group tae do it. But I want tae hear yer ideas first. I shall speak last, plagiarist that I am, and, Michael, I want ye tae remember it all for posterity. Now, Peter, begin. Ye're the host."

"No, Agatha is," protested the good husband, "this is her party."

"Then Agatha, *begin*," boomed Shivas.

"No, Peter is the one with ideas," said our handsome hostess, and everyone began talking at once.

Eventually Peter began. "All right, my friends," he said, leaning forward and looking round at us all, his graying temples reflecting the candlelight. "I'm not an intellectual sort like the rest o' ye, so ye're not goin' tae get any fancy theories from me. And I'm goin' to keep this speech very short, for I'm sayin' my farewell to the game. I've suffered enough with it."

Peter's seemingly decisive statement was met with a round of hoots and gibes. Apparently he had made such renunciations before. "Let us drink a toast to Peter's imminent departure," said Shivas, lifting up his glass, "and to his predictable retoorn." There was a round of laughter as we all lifted glasses toward our host.

Kelly got up from the table and went into the sitting room. He returned with an old wooden-shafted club that was taped together with wads of black binding tape. "Break it noo," he said, offering the golfing stick to his father, "it'll bring everyone luck."

Peter smiled and took the club with both his hands. His face was bright red now from drink and what seemed to be a sudden embarrassment, "Ye see, ma friends," he said, holding up the stick, "we call this our wishbone. Ye can each make a wish." Then he stood up and broke it with an enormous crack across his knee. He stood at the end of the table, sheepishly holding up a broken piece in each hand. "We do this, ye see, whenever I give up the gemme. Did ye make yer wishes?" There was another round of laughter and our host sat down.

The surprising performance had happened so swiftly that I had not had a chance to make a wish. But the first thought that had flashed in my mind, I can still remember it, was an image of a golf pro at the Salinas club who had come from Oklahoma, a colorful man with gigantic temper, throwing a sand wedge at me by mistake. It whirled like a vicious helicopter blade as it came right for my face—I ducked and it grazed my scalp. It was the closest I had come to being killed or maimed and now the image had surfaced as Peter broke his club.

"What did ye wish, Mr. Murphy?" Kelly asked in his whisky brogue from the other end of the table.

"That no one kills me with a golf club," my reply popped out. Everyone thought it was a great wish.

"Ye see, that is why I *break* my club." Peter grinned. "To save ye all from disaster."

"Oh, McNaughton, ye'll be back," Shivas's voice resounded above the rest, "but finish yer speech." The rest of the group urged Peter to continue.

"Awright, I'll tell ye what I think, for through my sufferin's a certain understandin' has developed." He looked with sad eyes around the table and winked at Julian. "If I've learned one thing about the game it is that 'tis many things to many people, includin' the many ones in my very own head." He tapped his temple. "We've certainly seen them come and go through Burnin'bush. Tall ones, short ones, scratch players, and duffers from the end o' the wardle. Intellectual sorts and workin' men, pleasant tempraments and mean ones, the MacGillicudys and the Balfours, the Leviases, the St. Clairs, the Van Blocks, the gentlemen from Pakistan— in terms of origin and character and ideas, a most diverse and complex lot. For each has his peculiar understandin', his peculiar theory, his peculiar view o' the world, his peculiar swing, God knows. Get them here on the links, and all their parts fall oot." He smiled sadly again and shook his head. "Gowf is a way o' makin' a man naked. I would say tha' nowhere does a man go so naked as he does before a discernin' eye dressed for gowf. Ye talk about yer body language, Julian, yer style o' projectin', yer rationalizashin', yer excuses, lies, cheatin' roonds, incredible stories, failures of character—why, there's no other place to match it. Ye take auld Judge Hobbes, my God, the lies he told last week about that round o' his in the tournament, 'tis enough to make ye wonder about our courts o' law. So I ask ye first, why does gowf bring out so much in a man, so many sides o' his personality? Why is the game such an X-ray o' the soul?

"Now let's take this thing ye call projection," he looked again at Dr. Laing. "One man sees the Burnin'bush Links as a beautiful thing, the next sees it a menacin' monster. Or one man'll see it friendly one day and unfriendly the next. Or the

same hole will change before his very eyes, within minutes.
What d'ye call that ink-blot test, Julian?"

"A Rorrshock, Peter, that's what ye're talkin' aboot."

"Yes, a Rorrshock, that's what a golf links is. On some days
I love these links of ours, on others I hate them. And it
looks different, by God, it *looks* different dependin' on my
mood. Agatha heer says I go through the same kind o'
trouble with her, guid woman." He reached toward his wife.
"Like marriage it is, like marriage!" The idea seemed to have
struck him for the first time. He and Agatha looked at each
other in silence for a moment. The sounds of silverware striking plates and the slurping of broth quieted as the two of
them exchanged secret knowings. All heads turned up from
the dinner and looked to the end of the table. Peter and
Agatha were sharing untold numbers of insights and feelings
regarding the relationship of golf and marriage, and the
group seemed to be awed by the sight. Six faces waited ex-
pectantly in the candlelight.

"Just like marriage," Peter said at last, in a quiet solemn
voice. Then he turned toward us with a small boy's smile of
discovery. "Why, Agatha's like a Rorrshock too." There
seemed to be a dozen "r's" in the word Rorschach. "Just like a
Rorrshock," he said again, turning back to look at her with his
child-like smile. "Marriage is a test of my devotion and my
memory that things will be all right."

Words of approval and congratulations sprang from all
sides of the table. We all wanted to cheer them on. I could
see that Agatha was his mother and young lover and God
knew what other incarnations in the Rorschach he saw. The
same complexity seemed to be true for her.

"A good marriage is as rare and complex and fragile as the
world itself," said Shivas, "and very like the game o' gowf.
Ye're right, Peter, ye're right." I remembered that he was a
bachelor and wondered if he had ever been married.

Then our host and devoted husband broke into an impas-
sioned speech comparing marriage to golf. The connection

had sprung some trapdoor of insight and lyricism in his heart, and all his sufferings and enthusiasms poured forth. Like golf, marriage required many skills, he said, "steadiness of purpose and imagination, a persistent will and willingness to change, long shots and delicate strokes, strength and a deft touch," the metaphors were tumbling in all directions now, "good sense and the occasional gamble, steady nerves and a certain wild streak. And ye've got to have it *all* goin' or the whole thing goes kaflooey." He clenched his fist and turned his thumb down. "Any part o' the game can ruin the whole. Ye've got to have all yer parts and all yer skills, yer lovin' heart, yer manhood, and all yer subtleties. Not only are ye naked to yerself and to yer partner, but ye've got to contend with yer entire self, all yoor *many* selves. Nowhere have I seen the Hindoo law of Karma work so clearly as in marriage and in golf. Character is destiny, my friends, on the links and with yer beloved wife." He took Agatha's hand and they exchanged unspoken thoughts again. "Get me another glass o' whisky, darlin'," he said, "this clarity is frightenin'."

Perhaps the insight regarding marriage or perhaps the whisky Agatha brought him cast another light on the game for Peter. Like a barometer of his mood, his complexion had become bright red again with pleasure.

"There is somethin' benign about the game after all," he said expansively, "we can read it in our history. It's recorded that after the Treaty of Glasgow in 1502, which ended our worst wars wi' the English, James the Fourth bought himself a set o' clubs and balls. The prohibitin' laws against the game, which he had renewed because the fields were needed for war practice, were dropped tha' year since there would be nae mair fightin'. Then he married Margaret Tudor the followin' year—bought himsel' some clubs and married the daughter of the English king—wha' d'ye think o' that! Marriage and golf again, both recorded for posterity! 'Tis curious, ye'll have to admit, that all o' this has been remembered in our history books."

Some of us asked how he knew all that. "He reads all he

can about the game," said Kelly, "thinks he'll finally read the secret."

"Now I've often thought about James the Fourth," Peter went on undeterred, "how he signed that treaty and bought himself those clubs. Reminds me o' President Eisenhower." He looked at me. "It's not a warlike man that loves the game so much." I felt constrained to say that Ike was getting a lot of criticism for all the time he was spending on the course. "Well, I'll admit that a man like that could get more done, but at least he probably willna' get ye into wars or silly ventures, seein' how much time he needs for his leisure. I think the very *thought* o' liftin' that prohibitin' law led James the Fourth to sign the Glasgow treaty. He couldna' have played unless the war was over, since they needed all that links-land for practicin' their bows and arrows." Julian Laing and Shivas both laughed at this proposal.

"Yer history's a Rorrshock," the old doctor rumbled with a smile that revealed several golden teeth. "O' course history aye has been."

But the challenge only seemed to fuel our host's passion for his subject. He claimed that men who loved games "did not have to use other human beings for their sport"—or lord it over private lives and morals. After the union of the Scottish and English crowns, James Six and One proclaimed that Sunday sports were to be permitted in Scotland. Peter recited a declaration by the king, which he had memorized, something to the effect that on Sunday "our good people be not disturbed or discouraged from any lawful recreation such as dancing, leaping, or vaulting." Those good Presbyterians could now leap about the streets after divine service. "And, moreover, that was the year the featherie ball was invented!" he exclaimed. "A ball that could fly further than any before it." The coincidence of those two events—the discovery of the "featherie ball" and the relaxation of the sabbath prohibition against sport—was significant, for every improvement in leisure got into laws and treaties and politics generally. The first international golf match, between the Duke of York (later James the Second of England and Scotland) and John Patersone, the shoemaker, against two English noblemen, "a match much remembered and in the spirit of the Restoration," was held at the Leith Links sometime later in the century; its importance as a public event showed how games encouraged the meeting of men in a peaceful manner. He said that the house John Patersone built with his winnings from the match still stood in Edinburgh, that we could all see it for ourselves. Then he talked about the first golfing societies, the competition for the silver club at Edinburgh, and "the banding together of the brothers." With the English wars lessening, Scotsmen could now join to fight the elements and the "demons of their souls" at the Royal Aberdeen Club, the Royal and Ancient Club, the Honorable Company of Edinburgh Golfers, or the Musselburgh Club. All these fraternities made their rules, started their competitions, adopted their emblems and uniforms. Black jackets, red jackets, tartan jackets, and even more colorful outfits became obligatory for club festivities and play on the various golfing links. "Ye were fined if ye didna' wear the uniform—and why was that?" he asked. "To form a band o' brithers, that's why. *It was a way for men to join in peace and mak' it vivid to themselves.*" He pounded fiercely on the table for emphasis, rattling the dishes. "About the time o' the first clubs even the English and Scottish parliaments joined together, completin' what the Treaty o' Glasgow started two hundred years before. So ye see, at every important joinin' o' the English and the Scots golf played a part. At the very least, the memory of these great events of golf and politics were joined in our memories and imaginations and history books. Now extend this to all the history o' games and leisure. In golf our spears —and my friends, the Scots have had some fierce ones—get beaten into gowfin' sticks. Now we would beat the good earth instead of our fellow man."

At about this point in the conversation, I told the group about my friend Joe K. Adams' proposing a Gymnasium for the Production of Dionysian Rites and other Health-Giving

Rituals. Adams claimed that body chemistry was altered during wild dancing and other emotional sports. He claimed that dancing helped the bodily functions in general and opened up the mind. Julian thought it was a good idea. He had developed a theory that certain kinds of psychosis came from a lack of proper exercise.

"Better games would empty entire wings o' oor mental 'ospitals," he said in his broad Scots burr. His wispy silver hair glowed like a halo in the candlelight, giving his face an iridescent quality. "I've cured several myself with nothin' mair than games and dancin'. And listenin' to the pipes can blow the mind free, too." He then described the "perfect golf links." It would include music on certain holes. All sports, he said, are improved when you can hear the right music, with the inner ear if possible, or with bagpipes and bands if you couldn't. Ecstasy produced beneficial vitamins, it seemed.

"Oor brain is a distillery, pumpin' strange whiskys into the bloodstream to produce a permanent intoxication. Ye've got to feed the right things to the distillery, or ye get some bad green whisky." He made a retching sound and spit into his plate to emphasize the point. Eve Greene flinched and Adam pretended not to notice.

"But not gowf, Julian," Peter broke into the old doctor's speech, "not gowf. Gowf is for quietin' the mind, not stirrin' it. Look what happened when ye sent poor Campbell aroond the links with that dancin' step ye showed him. The members wanted to lock him up." Apparently Julian had prescribed an eighteen-hole Highland Fling for one of his patients.

"Oh, oh, oh." Julian leaned away from the table and his voice rose, "but look wha' happened to the man. 'Twas a cure, wouldna' ye say?"

Peter and the others agreed it had been a cure. Campbell had eventually gone off to the South Seas to write a book. But the argument continued. Peter and the Greenes took sides against Julian, maintaining that the beauty of the game lay in its poise and decorum, in its Apollonian virtues. The fierce old doctor took the Dionysian line; the game was meant for dancing, he said. "Noo look at ye, Peter, ye play against yer emotions, with yer emotions, through yer emotions. Wha' about the names ye have for yer different selves?" It was true. Peter McNaughton, like many others, had different names for his different golfing selves. I cannot remember them exactly, but they went something like "Old Red," for a mean and choleric one that broke clubs and swore viciously at his wife; "Divot," for a spastic one dangerous to onlookers; "Palsy," for another with floating anxiety, tremors of the hands and huge nervousness on the first tee. He seemed to have a certain detachment about them, referring to them as if they were familiar presences. He talked to them apparently. Agatha and Kelly knew who they were. Dialogues were held with them at dinner. Peter was a foursome all by himself.

"Tae me," said Julian, "yer a livin' example o' what the game is all about. What is it but the comin' together of our separate parts? Ye said it yerself, Peter, just a little while ago when ye compared the game to marriage. Our inner parts want to marry too."

I looked at Agatha. She was nodding in agreement, like many wives I have seen who pray for their husband's integration. Her hands involuntarily formed a prayerful attitude.

"Well, 'Naught' has taken ower noo," said Peter with sudden vehemence. I think he sensed the group was ganging up on him. "There is nae mair gowf while 'Naught' is in command." He had rejected these uncontrollable sub-personalities, along with golf and the whole business. Julian asked him what was left. "Oh, my friends, this lovely family, my sanity, my peace o' mind," he said with unconvincing gusto.

"Now, Peter 'Naught,' I think yer many sel's will return ere long over another game, over another dinner, in the midst o' this very family. There is nae banishin' them," said Julian with a sinister smile.

Peter was getting angry. He rose from the table. "Here, poor gowfin' addicts," he said, "drink up and arm yersel's against yer madness. I've said my piece. Ye can see I love the game, have my theories just like you, even my historical under-

standin's. But I'm leavin' it all behind. We will heer nae mair
o' 'Palsy' and 'Divot.' " There was a finality in his voice that
none of us wanted to question. It was someone else's turn
to speak.

Agatha proposed that we go into the sitting room; perhaps
she sensed that we needed a respite from so much talk. We
found seats for ourselves while Peter stoked the burning logs.
For a moment there was silence. There was a hint of embarrassment as we looked around at each other. Shivas spoke
up first. "Now, Adam," he said, "ye've been tellin' us about
yer theories the night, heer's yer chance. I ken they're
goin' tae be guid ones." We all looked at the little man, who
was almost invisible now in the shadows of the couch. I
remember hoping that he would make a long speech that
would give me some ideas for my own. But his enthusiasm
and bouncy spirit seemed to have left him; he looked at us
shyly as if he were afraid to say anything. We all sensed his
discomfort. When he finally spoke his voice was so low none
of us could hear what he said. Julian leaned forward with a
hand cupped to his ear. "Wha' was that, Adam," he asked,
"wha' was that ye said, did ye say the supermind?"

Adam nodded. It was painful to watch his embarrassment
but we still wondered what he had mumbled. The entire
group turned toward Julian. "What did he say?" someone
asked.

"I think he said that golf is the *supermind*," the old man
answered, scratching the back of his head. We all turned
back to Adam. The bashful little figure whispered another
inaudible sentence. We all turned to Julian again, as if he
were our interpreter. The old man shook his head and leaned
toward Adam. "Adam, ye'll have tae speak up," he said. "Did
ye say the *supermind*?"

The little man raised himself an inch or two on the couch
and spoke again. We could barely hear him. "Golf is the new
yoga of the supermind," he said.

"Good man!" Shivas exclaimed. "I can see that I'll enjoy
this." Apparently he was the only one who understood. Ev-

eryone else looked puzzled. Then Adam sank back into the shadows of the couch. It was going to take more encouragement to get him going in earnest. Eve reached over and put a reassuring hand on his arm.

"Well, now, that's certainly an interestin' beginnin'," said Julian. The rest of us nodded in agreement. There was still no response from the declivity in the couch.

"The yoga of the supermind," someone said as if he were just comprehending the meaning of the phrase, "yes, I see what he means."

I felt myself nodding in agreement. Yes, the yoga of the supermind. Yes. Yes, I see. . . .

Then Adam spoke again. The only words I could hear distinctly were "the next manifesting plane." I closed my eyes to ponder the gnomic phrases. There must be something to them, Shivas certainly seemed to think so. Supermind, a term from Aurobindo, but golf being "the yoga of the supermind," that was a little hard to follow. And "the next manifesting plane," what was that? As I pondered thus I heard a small commotion across the room. I opened my eyes and lo!—there was Adam standing on the couch. He stood in the flickering shadows bouncing gently on the cushions of his seat. Then he began to speak. "Golf recapitulates evolution," he said in a melodious voice, "it is a microcosm of the world, a projection of all our hopes and fears." I cannot remember all the phrases, but his words were an ecstatic hymn to golf, not golf the game I knew, but golf as it might appear in the Platonic World of Ideas, the archetypal game of games. As he talked I wondered what his course in "cosmic ecology" must be like. No professor of mine at Stanford had ever talked like this.

He told about the technological changes in the game and how they brought new powers and awarenesses into play for those who pursued it with a passion. With its improved clubs and balls and courses, golf reflected man's ever-increasing complexity. It was becoming a better vehicle for training the higher capacities. And so it was becoming the yoga of the supermind, the ultimate discipline for transcendence.

As he gave this incredible speech I wondered if he played the game himself. Being no taller than five feet four, he must have had a difficult time if he did. I wondered how far he could hit the ball, if he could reach a green in regulation figures.

"Golf is played at many levels," he was almost chanting now as he swayed in the firelight. "Take our love of the ball's flight, the thrill of seeing it hang in the sky." He made a sweeping gesture with his arm, tracing an imaginary trajectory against the fire's glow. "How many games depend upon that thrill—archery, football, golf—the thrill of a ball flying to a target, have you felt it? The ball flying *into* the target; it's a symbol, of course. And here, friends, my theory leads . . .", he stepped down from the couch and crossed the room to the fireplace, ". . . my theory leads to the simultaneity of past and future. For everything has a past *and* future reason for being. Projectiles for example, our urge to see them fly is derived from our paleolithic past, from the hunt, we love to see the spear or stone in flight. But," he stood on tiptoes and his voice rose, "it is also an anticipation. The flight of the ball, the sight of it hanging there in space, anticipates our desire for transcendence. We love to see it curve in flight as if it is free—why else do we hit a fade or draw? We love to see it hang there, that is why we love to hit our drives so far. The ball in flight brings dim memories of our ancestral past *and* premonitions of the next manifesting plane."

He rocked slowly back and forth, occasionally making a wide, sweeping gesture with an arm. We were all staring at him now with amazement. "The thrill of seeing a ball fly over the countryside, over obstacles—especially over a stretch of water—and then onto the green and into the hole has a mystic quality. Something in us *loves* that flight. What is it but the flight of the alone to the alone?"

He was tilting back his head and his black eyes were dancing. One sensed that his shyness had given way to a passion tinged with madness. A few moments before I had wanted to draw him out and give him support, now I was beginning to think we should try to slow him down. He was not the first person I had seen grow strangely intense while attempting to account for the game's mystery.

"The theory of golf," he continued, "which Eve and I have evolved, is the most elaborate and complete one ever invented to account for the game. I think it explains *everything*."

I was suddenly aware of Julian. He was frowning and glancing from time to time at Shivas. I wondered what he saw in Adam's behavior. He had said that he was generally in favor of madness, but now he looked concerned. Though I was fascinated by the speech emanating from the fireplace I was glad we had a doctor around.

"Have you ever pondered the mystery of the hole?" the swaying figure asked. "What are its past and future connotations? Think about that one. And a *hole-in-one*, have you ever thought about that!" He looked around at us with a wide-eyed look full of portent. "A *hole-in-one*," he intoned the term as if it were the holy of holies, "the flight of the alone to the alone."

Julian turned in his armchair to look at Shivas. "Ye incourage 'im in this kind o' thinkin' now and ye see where it leads 'im." Shivas did not answer; he only looked at Julian with a grave inscrutable look. The old man turned back to Adam. "The flight o' the alone to the alone, do ye equate the average gowfer wi' Plotinus noo? It's a dim connection, Adam."

"But it's *so real*," the little man answered solemnly, with a glint in his eye. He stood on the hearth as if to get more height into his words. "All of our experience is full of anticipations, we love what we might be. That is why we love a low-sailing two-iron or a three-hundred-yard drive."

I wondered if he had ever hit a two-iron shot like the one he described—or a 300-yard drive. He was indeed describing the Platonic Game of Golf. "We know in our bones what we are meant to be, so we are attracted by any glimpse of greater possibilities. There are moments in every golfer's game when he gets off a Promethean shot or when he feels a marvelous state of mind. Do you know what I mean?" he asked, suddenly looking down at me.

I thought of my shots on the back nine that day and nodded, in spite of my fears for him. Yes, I knew what he meant, how could I forget? There was logic in his madness.

"Some players embody that feeling," he said in his melodious voice. "Bobby Jones did. If someone else does, we will love him too. So . . ." he paused in mid-sentence as if pondering the next turn of his thought ". . . so because evolution is always at work, golf is becoming a better and better vehicle for it all."

This last generalization was all Julian could take. "Humbug, it's all humbug," he growled. "There is nothin' awtaematic about evolution or gowf or any other thing. Adam, it's you that's awtaematic when ye talk like that."

I was surprised at the old doctor's anger and direct confrontation to Adam's logic: my impulse had been to listen and hope for the best. But Adam now had too much passion to be deterred. He launched into another line of reasoning about the inevitability of life's unfoldment, arguing that any human activity that received the investment golf did was bound to reflect more and more of the human situation with all its hopes, fears, loves, ways of coping, struggles for survival, aspirations for God—the works. Therefore, it had to reflect the always upward tendency of life. "Golf is a microcosm of the world," he said. "When you invent new clubs, you get new attitudes. Replacing divots only began when courses were built from scratch instead of being marked off across links-land. Replacing the divot means a change in consciousness. . . ."

"Now, Adam," Julian broke in, "ye dinna' mean tae tell me tha' the replacin' o' the divot shows an improvement o' the spirit. It only shows *me* that the herds o' public gowfers realize they're about to overrun wha's left o' the green." Peter nodded in agreement. The two of them were a dour contrast to Adam's incredible optimism.

But Adam Greene sailed on. "I look for signals of transcendence in golf as in everything else." He smiled triumphantly and stepped down off the hearth. "I ask you to think about your own experience. If you are honest—even you, Julian, you—will have to admit that I'm right."

"If I'm goin' to be honest, Adam Greene," Julian replied, "then I've got to talk about the signals o' the damned along wi' the signals o' transcendence. Ye can see any signals ye want in the game."

"Well, Julian, if you had eyes to see . . ." Adam threw his hands up.

"But there is more to it," Eve Greene interrupted, coming to her husband's rescue. They had talked so much about these things, these speculations were so important to them. Their eyes shone in the firelight. "The environment is so crucial," she said. "Our playing partners, the course, our state of mind, our whole life affect our game so much. Whenever we play Burningbush we feel something special, the kind of thing Shivas and Seamus talk about. We think the thirteenth hole is haunted."

Haunted? I thought of my own experience there. "Who is Seamus?" I asked.

"We'll not be bringin' Seamus MacDuff into this," said Peter vehemently. "I can't stand the man."

"Now, Peter," said Shivas, "now, Peter—Seamus is our great good friend." He smiled at our host and reached over to squeeze his arm.

"Who is Seamus MacDuff?" I asked the question louder this time.

"Seamus MacDuff," said Eve Greene, "is the local madman, or a very *wise* man, depending upon your point of view. He and Shivas are very special friends."

"Who is he?" I persisted. There seemed to be no end of strange characters in this innocent-seeming town.

"Well, Ah'll tell ye, Michael, if ye promise to keep it a secret noo," Shivas fixed me with a solemn look. "Seamus

MacDuff is the man who invented the game so long ago. He's workin' on it still, perfectin' it ye might say. And blessin' our town here by choosin' our links to do his special work." He leaned toward me. "And Seamus it is who teaches me most o' what I know about the game."

There was a long silence. The ghost of Seamus was with us. I began to wonder if I had seen him on the course. I seemed to remember a seedy-looking character walking back and forth along the far edge of that treacherous ravine on the thirteenth hole. Then—weird sensation—I realized I *had* seen him! The glimpse I had gotten had not been important then, absorbed as I was with our play. But now I remembered him vividly. I could have sworn he was wearing a tattered black tail coat! "Did we see him on the thirteenth?" I whispered to Shivas.

"Noo did ye see him there!" he answered loudly, pulling back from me with a wide-eyed look. "Did he speak?"

"Well, he did seem to be saying something," I answered. To my amazement I now remembered that he *had* spoken. "But I can't remember what he said," I went on vaguely.

Had he been talking to us? How could I repress such a vivid perception? I had been totally preoccupied with my game after Shivas's strange performance and my own extraordinary shot. But to have my recognition of Seamus Mac-Duff totally obscured. . . . At that point I asked Agatha to get me another glass of whisky. There was a long silence. Finally Shivas spoke.

"I like yer theories, Greenes," he said. "Speakin' o' environments, I've aye wanted to play at the Tuctu gowf course in Peroo. 'Tis the highest in the world, they say. 'Tis said tha' the game is played there from mountain top to mountain top. There wid be yer environmental effect, now widn't? The ball wid fly a mile."

"I thought ye wanted to play in Tibet," said Kelly.

"Well, Tibet [he pronounced it Ti'but] wid be a place a'right, but this is the worst yeer in their history and I dinna' think we'll have much o' a chance tae do it," he said gravely. That was 1956, the year the Chinese overran Tibet. I learned that this had affected him deeply. "But gowf has been played there, o' that we can be shair noo." He said this last with great conviction.

"I always said ye shoulda' played wi' the Sodom and Gomorra' Gowfin Society on the Dead Sea," rumbled Julian from the depths of his armchair. "Noo there yer ba' would nae 'ave gone very farr," he rolled his r's as if he were savoring them. "Nae verry farr at a'. Twelve hundred feet below the sea, their li'l coorse was. Played the thing maself before the war. Like playin' in the inferno. The inferno itself. Only the English woulda' thought of doin' a thing like tha'."

"The Sodom and Gomorrah Golfing Society!" Eve exclaimed. "There was such a place?"

"Indeed there was, in a town called Kallia, upon the Dead Sea," Julian said.

"Now, Julian, you must admit that playing such a course affected your game," said the pixilated lady, ever hopeful for her husband's theories.

"Well, I'll tell ye, Eve," he replied, "it left an indelible impression on me that the English could stick it out in hell and niver know the difference."

The whisky now was having its effect, and the conversation bobbed along as if we were shooting the rapids of the Colorado. Adam and Eve continued to elaborate their sweeping theory of evolution. They talked about successive levels of mind, the opening up of supramental powers and awarenesses, and somehow came around to gardens. "The history of golf and the history of gardens are interlocked," they said. "The golf links here in Burningbush are an exploded garden." Then they explained the relationships between gardens and certain states of mind, how the English made the formal European gardens more like nature, made them gentler and more random. I said that nothing in England or Scotland could rival Pebble Beach for sheer grandeur, that the famous

California golf course should certainly produce some wonderful states of mind, though I had never heard of any actually occurring there. Then the conversation came round again to Seamus MacDuff.

"He's an embarrassment to the city and a royal pain in the ass," said Peter abruptly. "Why they let him live out in that ravine, I'll niver know."

"Does he actually live out there?" I asked.

"Let us say he spends a good deal o' his precious time there," said Shivas. "He's studyin' the game at all times, workin' on his theories o' the wardle."

It was uncanny how much I could remember now about that scroungy-looking character. I seemed to remember him gesticulating in our direction as he walked along the far edge of the gully.

"It's reputed that he's writing a book which will be published after his death," said Eve. "But no one knows for sure."

"Oh, he's mad as a loon and why d'ye all pretend to take him so serious?" said Peter. "Ye're makin' fun o' him just like everybody else. That's what ye're really doin', just makin' fun of him."

"I niver make fun o' the man," said Shivas gravely. "And he has a book indeed, a great book. *The Logarithms of the Just*, it's called, bein' first notes for a physics o' the spirit. I've seen it twice. So dinna' tell me that I'm makin' fun of 'im, Peter. He's my truest teacher."

"What kind of theories does he have?" I asked, my curiosity growing with each statement.

"Apparently he's studying gravity," someone said. "His theory explains the alignment of human consciousness with the physical forces of the universe."

"Is he a mathematician?" I asked.

"In the Pythagorean tradition," said Shivas. "Ye see, Michael, he's had to tip the balance of his mind to study gravity. He's floatin' free now to get a better fix upon this world of ours." In a few hours I would discover Shivas's own formulations relating gravity to the subtle forces of the human soul.

"Seamus MacDuff is the one sane man among us," Julian slapped the arm of his chair. "The only sane man among us. In a world gone completely off the target he's readjustin' his sights. What if it takes a lifetime, are any o' us here doin' any better?" He scowled at us all. "The whole o' our world is gone off target. Now, I would like to say my piece about the game of gowf." He cleared his throat and spat into the fire. Then he began to speak in his richly cadenced, rumbling brogue, and summoned a vision of hell on earth. In attempting to recreate his monologue I have become aware once again that a vision can be communicated only by the person who has it. His words went something like this.

"Now see how spellbound we are by the wardle around us. Hypnotized from mornin' to night by every influence, human or otherwise, that impinges on our senses. Adam, ye talk about the grand evolution but despair yerself about our times. For every theory ye propose about the improvement o' the game, I'll show ye how the game is fadin' away, losin' its old charm, becomin' mechanized by the Americans and the rest o' the world that blindly follows them. Look at the crowded links, the lack o' leisure, the hurried startin' times, the ruination o' the old clubs where ye could gather with your friends and enjoy some good conversation. Where's the evolution in all o' that now, I ask ye? Show me where it is. Now my special angle on life is bein' a doctor, lookin' at people's ailments these fifty years. And I want to tell ye tha' the language o' the body says, help! help! help! There is no apparent increase o' longevity, health, happiness, or digestin' in the world as far as I can see. A chance for more to live all right, an elimination o' the plagues and epidemics, an end to infant deaths. But with all o' that nae increase in the higher goods o' life. We are all o' us hypnotized, I tell ye, and you're just refusin' to look at the facts if ye say it otherwise. Now gowf reflects all this, yer right, Adam. It does indeed reflect all this. But what an awful reflection! What an *awful* reflection," he shook his head sadly as he repeated the words. "I see the distorted swings, the hurried rounds, and now the electric carts tae ruin the courses and rob us of our exercise. And the configuration o' physique that shows me how our twisted lives twist our bodies. I don't think evolution is goin' ahead so much as just goin' along breedin' more unfitness every day. We have got off the mark, gone for the wrong things, forgotten what it's all about, gotten oursel's hypnotized by silly people. If it weren't for Shivas here, and Seamus MacDuff, I would say there's nae hope left at all." He then went around the room pointing to each person's foibles and source of unhappiness. He asked the Greenes about their constant hypochondriacal complaints—Adam's bad back, Eve's migraine headaches—all the complaining which punctuated their grand theories of the universe. And Peter McNaughton about his endless rushing—at work, at home, at play, his irritability over tiny frustrations, his compulsive avoidance of pleasure through most of the day. Even Shivas was not spared. Why, asked the forbidding doctor, did he have to rush about the streets in the early morning hours provoking theories that he was some kind of sexual offender? He ended with a horrendous blast at me. He could tell just by looking at me that there wasn't a fiber of dedication in my character, that I was a good American boy "pluckin' the fruits of an easy life." The line he ended with, the last twist of his conversational dagger, was an admonition that each of us compare our complainings and frustrations now with our sufferings ten years before. "It is interestin' to see how persistent the patterns are," he said. "And then we sit here, gettin' high on whisky, paintin' glorious pictures o' the higher life, while the world outside grows ever darker."

As the old doctor's black and eloquent harangue developed I became aware of Agatha McNaughton. She smiled at each person as their turn came for Julian's roasting. She had seen him do this before, I suspected, and would help carry her friends through it as she would a child who cried in the night.

She gave Shivas a long and affectionate look when his turn came. Then she winked at me. When Julian was finished she quietly rose and brought us each a cup of tea. It was a time for silent thought, so many of the old man's words had hit the mark. Eve Greene was furious, I thought, and had a difficult time returning Agatha's understanding look. Adam looked dumbly into the fire. Agatha permitted the silence, but was seeing to it that we were comforted through our dark reflections. Dr. Laing spit into the fire again and muttered a few inaudible curses.

Shivas was the first to speak. "Julian," he said solemnly, "ye've made it difficult for me to sing the praises o' gowf. There is somethin' like the final word about yer speech. I think we need Agatha's blessin' now if we are to proceed." He leaned toward her. "Now Agatha, lassie, tell us what ye think. Ye're the fairest one here, and the only one to break the spell tha' Julian has put upon us." His sentiment was echoed by the rest of the group. We all wanted her warmth after the pounding Laing had given us. So Agatha spoke about golf and about the love men have for one another.

"It's the only reason ye play at all," she said. "It's a way ye've found to get together and yet maintain a proper distance. I know you men. Yer not like women or Italians huggin' and embracin' each other. Ye need tae feel yer separate love. Just look—ye winna' come home on time if yer with the boys, I've learned that o'er the years. The love ye feel for your friends is too strong for that. All those gentlemanly rools, why, they're the proper rools of affection—all the waitin' and oohin' and ahin' o'er yer shots, all the talk o' this one's drive and that one's putt and the other one's gorgeous swing—what is it all but love? Men lovin' men, that's what golf is." The strong lines of her face were softened by the fire's glow. "I think the loss o' love is Julian's real despair, whate'er his philosophizen' tells him. He misses the leisurely pace when there was time for more affection. Now don't ye, Julian? I miss it too. Most of the women miss it, the ones I know. We hurry through our days." She looked at

Peter and took his hand. Then she lifted back her head. "Oh, golf is for smellin' heather and cut grass and walkin' fast across the countryside and feelin' the wind and watchin' the sun go down and seein' yer friends hit good shots' and hittin' some yerself. It's love and it's feelin' the splendor o' this good world." There was music in her gentle Scottish burr, a fullness in her feeling for us. It was becoming obvious by now that each of us had a different song to sing in praise of the mysterious game.

"Oh, Agatha, Agatha," said Shivas, "how can I say anything more after that? Yer eloquence leaves me dumb. It would be embarrassin' for me tae say anythin' at all, so I'll not speak. Good friends, let me be now. I'll just look into the fire and roominate about what ye've all said."

But his friends would not have it. They all urged him on. He protested again, but was drowned out by their urgings and derisions. "Humbug," rumbled Julian, "enough now o' yer habitual laziness. We willna' let ye git away wi' that." It was apparent that they knew what a put-on artist he could be.

"Well, now, what d'ye make o' that?" Shivas said. "Ye really value my poor views on the subject, it almost makes me want to weep." He smiled though as he said it.

And so his talk about golf began. He first asked Agatha some questions about what she had said, getting her to admit the game had its foul aspects as well as its noble and beautiful ones. He gave Julian credit for having stated so well the dark and tragic side, man's "hamartia" in golf and everything else. He got her to agree that people were usually hypnotized by the game, just as they were by most of the other activities in their lives, that Julian had been eloquent on that subject too. "But we must remember that hypnosis is first cousin to fascination," he said, "and all art and love depend on fascination. Ye can hear Beethoven playin' on the radio and not recognize it nor feel it at all if ye're preoccupied wi' somethin' else. But once ye turn to hear it, down ye go into his world, into his deep and stormy world. Or a poem bein' read by a friend, or a lovely face—if ye're not fascinated by it, it goes right by unnoticed. So it is with golf. There's no use playin' if the fascination doesna' take ye." He was silent for a while. "Now ye've brought in Seamus MacDuff, so I must tell ye what he tells me, him bein' my main teacher about the game. Accordin' to him, life is nothin' but a series of fascinations, an odyssey from world to world. And so with golf. An odyssey it is—from hole to hole, adventure after adventure, comic and tragic, spellin' out the human drama. Fascination holds us there, makes us believe 'tis all-important. Now, and this is the point Seamus makes so often and which I love so much, fascination has a gravity of its own. It can draw upon the subtle forces, draw them round us lik' a cloak, and create new worlds." He looked at me as he said this. Suddenly his face began to shimmer. I felt the same presence I had felt on the course with him. "Worlds of subtle energy when the fascination takes us," he said, drawing us into his spell. "Now this happens all the time, every day, and we go like Ulysses from place to place, hardly knowin' what we're about. But—and this is the second point from old Seamus's book—we can begin to look around and ken these many worlds, what they are and what they make us. World upon world, all the heavens and hells of our daily lives. 'Man the great amphibian,'" he began reciting from the *Religio Medici*, "'whose nature is disposed to live, not only like other creatures in divers elements, but in divided and distinguished worlds.' And his odyssey does not end here or there or any place we've seen yet." He paused again, gazing across the room as if waiting for the next inspiration. "So as we ken these many worlds, see them with a clearer eye, we learn to move more freely—and learn o' worlds tha' lie beyond." He raised a long finger and held it in front of his nose. "Yes, worlds within worlds right in front o' our nose. Think about the times ye really concentrated upon a thing, did ye see it change in front o' your very eyes? Now, did it not? The lovely face tha' grew lovelier still, the new music in the old tunes, the new meanin's in the familiar poem, the new energies in the old swing? Yes, worlds within worlds here, with new shapes, new powers.

Now did ye e'er make a ball curve in the air just by willin' it? New powers there, will ye na' say? So this is the first point o' my speech, my friends, namely that fascination frees our journey through the worlds and opens the doors to where we want to go. In this I think—when I get into my metaphysical mind—I think we're like the great God, who lost Himself in this dark unconscious universe and wends His way back toward light and fullest knowin'. Forgettin' and rememberin', losin' and findin' our original face—the great God and all of us are in the game togither. We're all o' us joined to the growin' world, with God we're wakin' up." There was total silence in the room now, except for the sound of logs snapping in the fire. Then a smile appeared on his face, it broadened to a grin, he began to laugh. "Oh, we forget and remember every day, forget and remember what we're all about. And so, my friends, we come to discipline and the loveliness o' rools, the very loveliness of the game o' gowf. Fascination is the true and proper mother of discipline. And gowf is a place to practice fascination. 'Tis slow enough to concentrate the mind and complex enough to require our many parts. In that 'tis a microcosm of the world's larger discipline. Our feelin's, fantasies, thoughts and muscles, all must join to play. In gowf ye see the essence of what the world itself demands. Inclusion of all our parts, alignment o' them all with one another and with the clubs and with the ball, with all the land we play on and with our playin' partners. The game requires us to join ourselves to the weather, to know the subtle energies that change each day upon the links and the subtle feelin's of those around us. It rewards us when we bring them all together, our bodies and our minds, our feelin's and our fantasies—rewards us when we do and treats us badly when we don't. The game is a mighty teacher —never deviatin' from its sacred rools, always ready to lead us on. In all o' that 'tis a microcosm o' the world, a good stage for the drama of our self-discovery. And I say to ye all, good friends, that as ye grow in gowf, ye come to see the things ye learn there in every other place. The grace that comes from such a discipline, the extra feel in the hands, the extra strength and knowin', all those special powers ye've felt from time to time, begin to enter our lives."

I thought of our round that afternoon. "Those special powers and knowings," I knew what he meant. That drive on the first hole, curving gently to follow the path I had seen. The crystalline view from the thirteenth green, yes, I knew what he meant.

"My friends," he said, "devoted discipline and grace will bring ye knowin's and powers everywhere, in all your life, in all your works if they're good works, in all your loves if they're good loves. Ye'll come away from the links with a new hold on life, that is certain if ye play the game with all your heart."

Evanescent corridors of memory intervene between my writing and his talk, so there are gaps in this brief account. I remember well, however, the applause and hurrahs that followed and the magical presence he left in the room.

But this was not to be a gathering for contemplation. We were soon embarked on a lively discussion of shanking and the problem of evil; Peter, well influenced now by drink, maintained that in terms of body language it was the clearest example of the game's diabolical nature. Then suddenly there was a loud banging at the front door and raucous shouts from the street below. Someone was trying to get in. A large, ebullient man who looked to be in his late twenties came bursting into the room. He was dressed in an orange sweater and enormous red Tam O'Shanter. He demanded loudly that we join him in his revels. "Come on, ye sober logs," he bellowed, grabbing Peter's shoulders, "come to Clancy's house to celebrate my victory." He wrestled Peter around the room knocking over a chair. I was alarmed, he was so enormous. He must have been six feet five or so. He caught Agatha in a bear hug, then Kelly with a hammerlock around the neck. Then he saw Shivas sitting in a corner. "My God, look there," he cried, "who let him in, the hound of hiven, the bastard. He hounds me e'erywhere, the terrible man hounds me e'ery-where." He took off his Tam O'Shanter and sailed it across the room onto Shivas's lap. "A hole-in-one," he bellowed.

Shivas put the Tam on his own head and pointed a menacing finger at the intruder. "Ye'll na' disrupt our higher talk, Evan Tyree. We'er onto better things and will na' be led by you nor any man to celebrate mere victories o' the flesh."

Evan Tyree was the local golf champion, one of the best amateur players in British history, they said. When it came to scoring, he was the most proficient and famous of Shivas's pupils. He had just won a notable British tournament.

"My good friends, I've celebrated about the town wi' all the sober judges and potentates and will na' leave ye, the very arcane priests o' gowf. And ye'll na' tell me, Shivas Irons, to sober up—for God or any other one."

"Nae, nae, Evan, ye canna' end our party here," said Peter. "We've been singin' the praises o' gowf the night, each sayin' what it is that makes its mystery and allure, so now ye do the same. Tell us what the game means to you, great champion."

The rest of the group joined to urge the colorful intruder on. "Let's get the genuine word from a genuine champion," said Shivas. "Now we'll hear what it's really all about. Evan will put our poor talks to shame."

Evan Tyree walked across the room, grabbed the enormous Tam from his teacher's head and placed it on his own. "Let me wear my champion's crown if I must speak," he said. He drew himself to his full height and looked up at the ceiling. "But I winna' speak o' gowf, oh, no. I can only tell ye about my teacher, for 'twas he wha showed me the way." He bowed deeply, doffing his Tam to Shivas. " 'Twas he wha taught me a' the graces o' the gemme, to hold my temper when retreatin' from par and bogey, to use the inner eye to make the game a very prayer."

He held his hand to his chest. "When I was young and he was first a legend, I had the privilege o' playin' with him on many a day. And I wid throw my clubs and shak' my fist at God and scream across the links like a banshee. 'Twas he wha

showed me self-control. For he would miss his shots, deliberately I later learned, and stay so cool to embarrass me.
One day he shot a ninety, yes, a ninety, my friends, and
laughed and complimented me all the way. Had a grand
time, he did, never lookin' back at par, never panickin' or
cursin', just steady through it a', the same as he always is.
And that I say is the mark o' a brave and holy man, that he
can retreat like that from par without a whimper. I've never
forgotten that holy round, the memory o' it haunts me still
and settles me after many a rotten hole.

"And morower, 'twas he wha showed me the religion o' the
game. I'll ne'er forget the time he stood there on ol' thirteen
upoon the hill, for hours lost in contemplation, doin' his medi-
tatin' while standin' up. Jist a boy I came to watch him
there at sunset, and he stood into the wee hours, waitin' for
his inspiration. I learned a thing or two about the higher
laws tha' night watchin' him there lookin' out tae sea.

"And all the times I've tried to lead the man astray, a
hundred times, wi' bets and drinkin' and fornicatin', but there
he stands like the Rock o' Gibraltar, givin' in to his prayers
and contemplations but niver once tae me. Oh, we've gone
out on the town so many nights and howled at the moon
together and laft until the sun come up, but ne'er once did he
j'in me in my wretched time wi' the men and women o' the
town here. When we went to London I thought I would
corrupt him then, for once and for all. So I took him to the
greatest place in Mayfair, full o' the finest lassies o' England
and the Continent. I thought that night I would see him
fall but what d'ye think happened? He was the sensation o'
the house, regalin' fower or five o' the lassies wi' his stories
and winnin' smile, a regular satyer on the face o't. And disappear, he did, upstairs wi' a few o' them. But he winna' tell
me to this day what he did. Oh, he is a hard man when it
comes to deviatin'. Only in the upward direction will he go
astray."

"Enough now, Evan," Shivas broke in, "ye're only tryin' tae
rooin my reputation among the lassies, makin' me out tae be

some kind o' churchmoose. But we winna' be fooled by all o' that. It's my very own wildness that has so influenced you, just look at yer wild ways." Evan Tyree, I learned, was vastly erratic in tournament play and private life. Contemplation did not seem to be his calling. He picked Agatha up and fell with her in his lap onto the floor. "Now, Agatha darlin', ye're my true love, let's rin awa' frae Peter," he said and smiled drunkenly.

Agatha pushed him away. "Shivas is the only man I'd run away with," she said demurely.

"Oh, Peter, see that," Evan bellowed, "d'ye see that? The man steals the women too. Beats us on the course, steals the women, shows us up at philosophizen', a man to be contended with at every turn."

And so the party turned to raucous repartee. Evan and Shivas joined in a Highland Fling, while the rest of us sang "Munlochy Bridge" and "Devil in the Kitchen." They danced between the old crossed swords, which Agatha had taken from the mantel. They danced like two gazelles, locking arms, their heads almost hitting the ceiling as they jumped across the blades, their footwork flawless in spite of all the whisky. Then Peter emerged blowing his bagpipes, skirling "Scotland the Brave" with all its surging power, and we marched around the room, Julian leading the way, until Peter could blow no more.

Seamus MacDuff's Baffing Spoon

Around midnight we started slowing down. Julian slumped happily in his armchair, regarding us all with a benign look that betrayed the dark views of life he had been propounding. Agatha was urging him to go home, it being hours past his customary bedtime. No, he wanted just one more turn around the room, the old doctor said, but Peter's lungs had reached their limit. Gradually the party came to an end, and with hugs in all directions we tumbled out into the night. The McNaughton lights were the only ones on along the darkened street, and our voices—especially Evan's—bounced off the neighbors' houses until a shutter flew open and someone yelled at us to stop. The leader of our revel held his Tam in front of his mouth and waved good-by, as he swayed off down the hill toward Clancy's. Kelly managed to get Julian into the Mc-Naughtons' car to drive him home. Shivas and I were left alone in front of the house. "I'll walk ye to the Inn," he said, and we started off down the cobblestone street.

We walked along in silence, simmering in our alcoholic happiness. I was warmed by these new-found friends. I thought of Agatha and Peter asking me to return, their smiles as I looked up the stairs to say my last good-by, then Julian shaking my hand and asking me to forget some of the things he had said, and the Greenes insisting that I have their address in Cornwall. I knew I would remember that gathering for the rest of my life.

But then through the good feeling and warmth of friendship, through the alcoholic vapors, one thought intruded, one piece of unfinished business. How had I repressed that glimpse of Seamus MacDuff? I tried to remember whether he had said something, whether he had actually worn a tattered black tail coat as I seemed to remember. It was disturbing to think my memory and perception could be so unreliable. Something exceedingly strange had happened, yet I had forgotten it completely. I told Shivas what I was thinking.

" 'Tis nervous-makin' when yer mind does tricks like tha'," he said, "I know wha' ye mean." The more I let the memory develop the more certain I became that something very strange indeed had taken place on the thirteenth tee. Bolder now with camaraderie and whisky, I asked him why he had loosed that blood-curdling scream.

"Oh, that," he said quickly with a little smile and shrug, "I do that a lot on the thirteenth, tae scair away the divil." He turned and looked at me. "Did it disturb ye?" he asked innocently.

I said that it hadn't, seeing how I hit my approach. But he must have sensed that I wanted more explanation. He gave me a quick intense look, that sudden X-ray glance of his, then turned away. We walked along for another block or two until we turned into the street that led to The Druids' Inn, an old hotel I had found. He stopped and put a hand on my arm.

"Michael, have ye got a bottle in yer room or a cup o' tea?" he asked. "I feel like talkin'."

I said that I did and we went up to the little room I had taken for the night. To this day I can remember the excitement and sense of anticipation I felt then. I was sure he was about to take me into his confidence. But when we got to the room he simply stretched out on the bed and stared at the ceiling. I broke out a bottle of Perrier Water, something I carried with me all the way through Europe on that trip. I suddenly felt awkward being alone with him. After a few painful moments he broke the quiet.

"Tell me about yer trip heer," he said. He seemed utterly distracted, I could sense that he felt as awkward as I did.

And then one of those abrupt changes in my perception occurred. He suddenly seemed much smaller in stature. His face looked green and wizened in the room's dim light. I began telling him about my trip but the words were mechanical; I seemed to be watching the entire conversation from a distance. I told him about my interest in Eastern thought and contemplative practice, about Sri Aurobindo and the ashram in Pondicherry. I had a sense he was listening with half his mind.

"Do ye think ye'll stay at the ashram?" he interrupted. I said that I didn't know, that I might or might not depending upon what I found there. He studied me as I said it.

"Aurobindo believes in the earth—is that true?" he asked. The question surprised me. Apparently he knew something about the Indian seer, who was unknown in the Western world except to the most ardent students of Eastern thought. He jabbed his finger toward the floor for emphasis. "Is tha' true?" he repeated the question.

"Yes, he does," I replied, touched by the crude grasp he seemed to have of Aurobindo's thought.

"Well, how would ye like to meet Seamus MacDuff?" he asked. The rapid sequence startled me. Aurobindo, believing in the earth, Seamus MacDuff—I must have looked perplexed. He stood, regaining his expansive manner.

"Come, let us call upon Seamus in the midnight hour," he said. "And bring the Perrier Water." I hurried after him, a bottle of mineral water under each arm, wondering what adventure was coming next.

We found his car, a little Morris Minor, in front of his apartment a few blocks from the Inn. His head almost touched the roof as he got behind the steering wheel. With considerable coughing and sputtering the engine started and we shot off through the deserted streets. Burningbush locks up early, like most Scottish towns.

"The sound o' this machine is much discussed," he said as we careened around a corner. "Word o' this will certainly get out." He seemed excited. "Gi' me a slug o' tha' Perrier Water," he said as we roared through the night.

The oldest part of Burningbush Town adjoins the first and last holes of the links. One of the cobblestone streets in this section runs into a narrow grass-covered road that leads out into the golf course and then to the sea. We turned onto it and he shifted gears. "There are animals heer," he said, "all sorts o' animals." And indeed a pair of eyes gleamed in our headlight, then disappeared into the gorse.

"What was that?" I asked.

"Tha' was a banshee," he said decisively, as if he believed it.

We drove out slowly toward the thirteenth hole, bumping over the little-used road, both of our heads hitting the roof of the car. "Have you ever come out here before at night?" I asked. He did not reply as he concentrated on the potholes and gullies around us. He turned the little car off the road and stopped under a tree.

"From heer on, we walk," he said as he jerked the emergency brake. It was a windy night and I pulled the collar of my windbreaker up as we got out of the car, hunching my shoulders for warmth. Shivas spread his arms toward the sky and slapped his chest. "Hah, wha' a good idea," he said with gusto, "wha' a good idea." Still dressed in his white sweater, he seemed oblivious to the cold. He set out for Seamus's ravine at a half run, as if he knew every step of the way.

The golf course had a different look about it now. It seemed much more precipitous and full of jagged edges. Another pair of eyes appeared and hurried away. The wind made an eerie sound coming through the fields of gorse and sharp ravines, shrill, then deep like the sound of a drum. I could hear the surf booming in the distance.

We were descending into a gully and a small rock-slide started under my feet. I called out, asking him to slow his pace, but he had disappeared and there was no answer. Then as I started up the other side of the draw, something grasped my shoulder. It felt like a hand; to this day I could swear it was a hand. But as I jumped away there was nothing except an enormous boulder, a huge rock outcrop looming over my head. I sat on the rocky slope to get my breath. The impression of being grabbed had been so definite, I stared at the boulder until my heart stopped pounding. Then I heard Shivas calling down.

"Michael, where 'n the hell are ye?" his stentorian voice echoed through the howling wind.

I shouted back and started up the gully wall. He was standing at the top. "Something grabbed me down there, I could swear," I said as I joined him.

"Now, Michael," he said, "now, Michael, have another Perrier Water." I was still carrying one of the bottles. He squeezed my shoulder to reassure me. I jumped back. "That's just how it felt," I said.

He laughed at my fright. " 'Twas a banshee," he said with his big-kid grin. "They're harmless, completely harmless." He squeezed my shoulder again and started off toward the ravine. After he had taken a few steps he stopped, then split the air as he had done that day with a bloodcurdling scream. And then a second time—that eerie yodeling wail.

"God dammit, what are you doing?" I gasped.

"Gettin' rid o' the stale aiyer in my lungs," he shouted back at me through the wind.

"Jesus, can we slow down?" I gasped again. The rapid pace he was setting and the increasing weirdness of the situation had me shaking and out of breath. "Can we please slow down a minute?" I was almost pleading.

He stopped without looking back, put a hand to his forehead as if he were shielding his eyes against some invisible sun and peered into the darkness. I stood a few yards away from him and held my sides to get my breath back. The wind was howling and snapping the collar of my windbreaker around my ears. He turned in a semicircle as he scanned the inscrutable night.

"What are you looking for?" I shouted.

"Wha' do ya think?" he shouted back without turning to look at me.

Then, just as he uttered the words, the most God-awful sound began to rise from what I took to be the ravine. It sounded like a single high note from a gigantic organ, rising steadily in volume until it shivered the night. Then around it like sunrise came a massive chord of lower register, swelling to encompass the original note and spreading until it seemed to come from all sides at once. I ran up to Shivas's side and grabbed his arm.

"Jesus Christ!" I shouted.

He drew back and stared at me with what seemed to be astonishment. "What in hell's wrong now?" His voice had an edge of reprimand.

"That sound!" I cried. "That sound!"

"Oh tha'," he said loudly, pulling his arm away. " 'Tis the wind from the ravine. It means the comin' o' the northern lights."

As he said those words, the sound began to fade away, leaving the original high note wavering in the wind, as if it were echoing off the walls of some immense cathedral.

He glanced back to check my state, then started off again for the ravine at a half-run. My heart was beating wildly and I was still out of breath, but I stayed as close to him as I could, not knowing what would happen next.

Though we could see no more than 20 or 30 feet in any direction, I could tell from the bench and bag stand I had seen that afternoon that we were crossing the thirteenth tee. He slowed his steps and turned left toward the ravine. I shuffled along after him, feeling the ground cautiously with my feet.

Sensing the place again, I tried to summon my memory of where I had seen the strange old man. Where had I been standing? It might have been from the hill after we reached the green, or perhaps from this tee? The failure of my memory was unnerving. My shin hit a rock and I swore again—somehow the curses kept down my fear.

Shivas shouted one last time, then started down a rock fall into the ravine. It was pitch black below us. There was not the slightest sign of life.

We inched our way down the jagged incline, sliding at times in loose rock. The floor of the ravine was, I would estimate, some 40 feet below: it took us several minutes to reach it. As we climbed and slid through the rocks and dirt I could feel a growing stillness; the place was completely protected from the wind. When we got to the bottom I looked up at the boulders looming over us and wondered if we would ever get out.

"Seamus may not be heer," he said. "He woulda' answered us by now." He groped his way through the darkness up the gentle incline of the canyon floor. I stayed as close to him as I could in case another hand might reach out for me, swearing steadily as we inched along. We were coming to a wider place and the going was easier. I began to feel sand under my feet instead of gravel and dirt. He sat down on a rock. "Let's rest a minute heer," he said. "If he's around, he'll soon let us know."

We waited in silence for several minutes. My hard breathing and anxiety were subsiding and I began to discern the outlines of the cliff edge some 40 feet above us and the shape of the declivity we were in. As I grew accustomed to the darkness, I could see that there was a large open space around us. I ran my feet through the sandy dirt and wondered if anyone had played a golf shot from here to the thirteenth green. What would Seamus do if someone descended into his lair? I had an image of him scampering away like a frightened animal, like dirty old Ben Gunn in *Treasure Island*.

"Does he actually sleep out here?" I asked.

"In his cave over there," he nodded toward the wall of the ravine.

I peered through the darkness, but could see nothing, no cave opening or shelter of any sort.

"I can't see it," I said as I peered at the inscrutable rocks.

"Right there." He nodded toward the cliff again. Still I could see nothing. It occurred to me that Seamus might enter through some tiny hole.

There was a protected feeling under the looming canyon walls, a heavy feel to the air. We sat for several minutes savoring the stillness of the place. Shivas seemed abstracted, in a state like the one he went into before dinner. He sat looking at the sky, as he had on that window ledge. Watching him, I remembered Evan Tyree's story about the night-long trance so many years before.

He gazed at the starry sky for several minutes, then he pointed upward and asked if I saw a constellation of the zodiac (I cannot remember which it was). I said that I didn't; that the only things I could recognize were the Milky Way, the North Star, and the Big Dipper.

"I'm sorry," he said, "for I'd like to show ye somethin' ye've probably niver seen. It's the real zodiac, the true one. That there is Hogan." He pointed at a constellation he had named after the famous golfer and then at another named "Swilcan Burn." He traced the outlines he saw in the sparkling sky, but I could only see an amorphous mass of stars. "Too bad ye canna' see it," he shook his head, "it's too bad. Ye'll see it though if ye look a while."

Apparently he had discovered a new zodiac. He gazed up at it and began to hum a plaintive Irish melody. As I looked at the sky I saw an outline of Ben Hogan's Indian profile appear amidst the other constellations. It was the only one I could recognize besides the Big Dipper.

Shivas was silent again, then his resonant voice broke the stillness. "He's na' heer," he said decisively, "but let's wait a while in case he retoorns." He began rummaging about in the rocks around him, and in a moment had gathered some twigs and branches. He took a match from his pants pocket and ignited the little pile he had made. It took flame immediately. "I've aye been good at startin' fires." He smiled proudly. "Now find me some bigger pieces."

We built ourselves a rousing fire and settled down to wait

for Seamus. The towering cliffs were alive in the firelight. "Gi'
me some o' that Perrier Water," he said.

He leaned back against a rock and gazed reflectively into
the flames, as if he were willing to wait indefinitely. "Do you
think he might be asleep?" I asked. "Why don't we go look?"

"Oh, no"—he raised his hand in warning—"niver do tha'—it
would distoorb him somethin' awful. I ken his ways. He's
na' heer, I tell ye, he's na' heer."

I asked him where Seamus might have gone, seeing what
an ungodly hour it was.

"He has another place he goes to upon occasion. But he
loves to work at night—that's when he can feel the things he's
studyin'."

"*Feel* them?"

"Feel them, tha' is what I sayed." He cocked his head
and looked at me gravely. "Ye're interested in 'im, aren't ye?
How would ye like to see his weapon?" Without waiting for
my answer he got up and went over to the rocks he had said
were Seamus's cave. In a moment he returned with a long
black gnarled stick that looked like a gigantic Irish shillelagh.
He was waggling it as if it were a golf stick. "This heer is
Seamus's club," he said, gazing at it fondly. He swung it at an
imaginary golf ball. "Would ye lik' to see it?"

He handed it to me carefully, holding it gently with both
hands as if it were carried on a velvet cushion. It was the
meanest-looking stick I had ever seen. Black and gnarled and
hard as a rock, it was about the length of a driver. On one
end there protruded a heavy burl with a flat face. It was a
golf club fit for a caveman. I waggled it as he had done and
swung it carefully to avoid hitting the ground. It swung
easily. I swung it again. It zipped through the air as if it were
perfectly weighted. I swung it three or four times more, it
seemed to swing by itself.

"Tha's enough," he said, abruptly taking it back. "Tha's
enough," and started swinging the thing himself, half a dozen
times as if he could not stop. "We must na' damage it on the
rocks heer," he said as he swung, "or Seamus 'll gi' me dread-

ful hell. But ye must see this." He put the club down and went over to Seamus's hiding place. In a moment he returned with two white objects about the size of golf balls. He carried them as he had the stick, as if they were on a cushion. "These are his balls," he said with a fond wry smile. "Look at them."

They had hard leather surfaces and felt lighter than ordinary golf balls. "They're featheries," he said, "real featheries from the ol' days."

"Featheries," I learned later, were the balls used until the middle of the nineteenth century when gutta-percha balls were introduced into play. They were made of feathers and leather and hardened by being soaked in brine. "Seamus uses them in his research," he said. "Found them heer in the ravine, he claims."

He stepped over to an open space with a sandy surface and put them on the ground. Then he pointed with Seamus's shillelagh down the ravine. "See tha' target there?" he said. I looked in the direction he was indicating and indeed there was a target, a white circle some 3 or 4 feet in diameter painted on the ravine wall. It was about 40 feet away from him, barely discernible in the wavering firelight. It reminded me of a photograph I had seen in the *National Geographic* of a paleolithic cave symbol used for magic hunting rites. "Now watch this," he said.

He placed one ball in front of him and took a stance with the shillelagh as if it were his driver. He waggled it carefully, holding it an inch or two above the ground, gathering his concentration as he had done through our round that afternoon. I felt the same suck of energy as he centered his attention on the ball, then his swing unfurled. The ball exploded from the club and flew into the shadows, hitting the target with a loud pop. He took his stance in front of the second ball and swung again, hitting the target right in the middle.

"Ye see that?" he said, turning to face me. "Ye can do it with a stick if ye concentrate." Then he paused and looked

GOLF IN THE KINGDOM

78

thoughtfully at the gnarled club. "O' course, this is not yer ordinary stick," he murmured.

He retrieved the balls and hit them into the target again. I sat by the fire and watched him. I had the impression he was somehow compelled to repeat the performance, almost as if he were in the grip of the club. It went on for fifteen minutes or more. He may have hit twenty or thirty shots, a strange figure in the shadows, like some ancient shaman firing his darts at the approaching buffalo.

At one point he turned and held up the shillelagh. "He calls this his baffin' spoon—the name he rimembers from his chile'ood. Says one club's all ye need to play the game."

I leaned back with my feet toward the fire and looked up the cliff. The rock formations above me curved and receded into grotesque shapes and seemed to move in the flickering shadows. I saw two horned birds flying upward, a row of human heads in profile staring dumbly at one another, and the crenelated cliff edge like the wall of our fort. I tried to imagine other shapes as the jagged rocks moved in the fire-light. At the very top, between the crenels in my fortress wall, I saw a face staring down at me. It was the face of an old man with a large frizzy beard, motionless like the imaginary faces below it. As I looked at it, I could make out other features—tiny squinting eyes, a look bright with curiosity, and a mad, gay little smile that seemed to relish what it was seeing. I cocked my head to one side to get another angle on it. Then I started back.

It *was* a face. It was Seamus MacDuff!

I jumped up and shouted at Shivas. "There he is!" I cried. "There he is!"

He was picking up his balls at the target. "Now, Michael, now, Michael," he said loudly, "calm yerself. Seamus'll niver come if ye carry on like that." He came over to me and looked up the cliff. "Now, where is he?" he asked. I pointed at the cliff edge, the face was still there. "See it?" I said loudly, jabbing my finger toward it. "Look where I'm pointing."

"I canna' see anything at all," he said impatiently, "where ye lookin' now?" He looked back and forth along the edge of the ravine. "I dinna' see a thing. The place is gettin' to ye."

The face was still there, staring down at me, I was amazed that he couldn't see it. "Look," I shouted, grabbing him by the shoulder and pointing so that he could see down the line of my arm.

"I dinna' see a thing," he said again. "I dinna' see a thing." Then he turned away and stood in front of the fire, rubbing his hands for warmth. "Michael, come heer," he said firmly. I turned away from the cliff. "Look at the fire," he said, "it'll calm ye doon." I raised my hands to feel the fire's warmth, shaken and still certain that Seamus was watching.

"How'd ye lik' to hit a few wi' Seamus's club?" he said quietly. He walked over to the open space where he had been hitting his shots and held up the shillelagh. "Come," he said, waving me toward him with an abrupt decisive gesture. I looked back at the cliff edge. The face was gone. I peered intently at the place where it had been, then scanned the entire perimeter of the ravine wall. There was no face to be seen.

"It's gone," I said.

"Ye see," he answered, "the fire plays tricks there on the rocks. Come hit a few."

I was relieved—and disappointed. I wanted to see the mysterious figure of Seamus MacDuff in the worst way by now.

He handed me the gnarled stick, cradling it on its imaginary cushion as if it were a scepter. I waggled the stick carefully, gradually lowering it into the arc of my golf swing until I was swinging it with a full sweep. It had amazing balance. "It's incredible how easily it swings," I said. "Did he make it himself?"

"Claims he made it from an old shillelagh." He was watching me with amusement. "Do ye want to hit one now?" Without waiting for an answer he teed up a featherie on the sandy ground. "Now, Michael," he said as he put the ball on a tiny mound of earth, "try to hit it clean without hittin' any rocks. Seamus'll gi' me royal hell if we hurt his baffin' spoon."

I eyed the primitive target and swung. The ball exploded from the club and I looked up to follow its flight. I could not see where it had landed in the dancing shadows.

"Ye missed the taraget," he said with a broad smile, "but ye hit it good. Seamus woulda' been proud o' ye. Heer, hit another one." He teed up the other ball.

I swung and hit it squarely. "Where did it go this time?" I asked, peering into the shadows.

"Ye hit it on the other side o' the taraget this time, but yer swingin' good." He was grinning broadly now. "Ye're the first person I've e'er seen wi' Seamus's club beside maself. Ye make a funny sight."

I held the shillelagh up in the light. "I feel funny holding it. I swear it wants to swing itself."

"Come, let's find the featheries," he said, walking off toward the target. I followed him down to the white circle. It was painted with some kind of whitewash. I could see that it had been painted over many times.

"Has he repainted this?" I asked, pointing to the crusty markings.

"Been usin' it for yeers. It washes off each winter in the rains." He picked up the balls and led me back to our imaginary tee. "Michael, come heer," he said, "I want to show ye somethin'." He had me take my customary golf stance in front of a ball he had put on the ground. "Now, I want ye to try somethin' slightly different this time, will ye do it?" He looked at me hopefully, cocking his head to one side. His large blue eyes caught the flickering firelight. I could see my reflection in them, he was standing so close, a distorted image of my entire body wavering like a flame. "Would ye like to try it?" he repeated the question, fixing me with that slightly cross-eyed double-angled look. I could now see two images of myself in the mirror of his eyes, each one slightly different from the other. I nodded that I was willing. "Awright, now," he said quietly, raising a long finger. "When ye swing, put all yer attention on the feelin' o' yer inner body—*yer inner body.*" He whispered these last words as if he were telling me a secret.

I looked at the shifting reflections in his eyes. To this day I can vividly remember my reaction. It was as if an immediate split occurred in my mind. A part of me instantly knew what he meant; another part began to question and puzzle. I looked at him dumbly, without answering, as the two attitudes formed themselves.

He leaned toward me and took my arms in his hands. "Close yer eyes," he said soothingly. Then he lifted my arms, I was still holding the shillelagh like a golf club, and moved them through the arc of an imaginary swing as a golf professional does with a student, whispering again the words, "feel yer inner body." My questions and puzzlement quieted and I fell into the rhythm of his movements, slowly swinging the club and sensing what he meant. It was like the state I had discovered that afternoon during our round of golf—a growing power, rhythm, and grace, a pleasure that had no apparent cause. Yes—perhaps you have had that sense of it—a body within a body sustained by its own energies and delight, a body with a life of its own waiting to blossom.

"Do ye see what I mean?" he murmured as he swung my arms back and forth. I nodded and he backed away. "Now try to hit the ball tha' way," he said.

I adjusted my stance and waggled the club, focusing my attention on the sense of an inner body. When I swung I topped the ball and it bounced high in the air.

He nodded with approval. "Good, good," he said loudly, "ye stayed right in it, now try another."

I took my stance and swung again. This time the ball flew toward the target but fell short. "Ye did it again. Good!" he said decisively. "Now stay wi' tha' feelin'." We found the balls and repeated the exercise. He seemed oblivious to the results as he studied my attitude and "energy." He claimed that my state of mind was reflected in an aura around me which he could sense. "Yer *energy* was good that time," he would say, or "it wavered on that one." He was as definite about these statements as he was about my physical form.

Our lesson continued for half an hour or more, some twenty or thirty shots, while I practiced that indubitable awareness of my "inner body."

The experience went through stages. At first there was a vague yet tangible sense that there was indeed a body closer to me than my skin, with its own weight and shape. It seemed to waver and bounce and subtly change its form, as if it were elastic. Then—I can still remember the feeling so clearly—it changed to an hourglass: my head and feet were enormous and my waist was as small as a fist. This sensation lasted while we looked for the balls and returned to our tee, then it changed again. My body felt enormously tall, I seemed to look down from a point several feet above my head. I told him what I was feeling. "Now come down heer," he said, calmly putting a finger on my breastbone. "Just come down heer." I returned to my ordinary size and shape, and continued swinging.

I was aware that part of my mind had suspended judgment, that many questions were simmering still. But it felt marvelous to swing that way, so absorbed in the pleasure and feel of it. And it was a relief not to worry about the results. I could have gone on for hours.

But he ended the lesson abruptly. "Enough for now," he said, putting a finger on my chest, "rimember the feelin'. Yer inner body is aye waitin' for yer attention." We added some branches to the fire, which had almost died out, and leaned back against a pair of rocks. I glanced up the cliff, but no face was there, just the writhing shadows on the canyon walls. I felt marvelously alive, as if I were floating in some new field of force, but the questions that had been suspended began rising like vapors. This state I was in was too good to be true, too easily come by, I began to wonder how soon it would fade after Shivas and his colorful admonitions were gone. Anyone would feel good around him, getting so much attention, being led into adventures like these. Dark and true premonitions, I felt an edge of sadness.

He must have sensed what was going through my mind. "Wha' ye thinkin' there?" he asked with a fatherly tone in his voice. "Tell me wha' ye're thinkin'." I told him some of my doubts. I especially remember asking him if all his talk of inner bodies and subtle energies wasn't a mere device for helping concentration. I told him about the Hawthorne experiment in which a group of social psychologists had found that workers in a factory had improved their output every time a change was made in their routine, no matter what that change might be. I asked him if he was running a Hawthorne experiment on me.

He leaned back with his genial grin and shook his head in mock exasperation. "They're two Michaels, I can see; Michael the plunger and Michael the doubter," he chided. "Wha' a shame it is tha' ye canna' even go five minutes heer without yer good skeptical mind intrudin'. Yer good skeptical mind, tha's a problem for ye." He raised his finger like a wand and shook it at me. "Watch out for yer good mind," he said.

I gave him some kind of argument, I am not sure of its exact content, but felt as I was doing it that some monotonous tape loop was running in my brain. I felt the excitement of our adventure, but the tape loop kept running. I asked him if Seamus MacDuff was insane, living in this ungodly ravine.

He gazed into the fire with melancholy amusement and began shaking his head. "Wha' yer sayin' tells me again tha' the world is na' ready yet for Seamus. To swing his *baffin' spoon* and still question the man . . ." He shook his head sadly. I felt chagrined. I was the first person to swing that stick besides Seamus and himself and now I was questioning it all. He was more vulnerable about this hidden world than I thought; I could tell he was hurt.

We were suddenly shy with one another. I was too much in awe of him to be reassuring; he was intimidated by my doubts and questions. I mumbled something about how good it felt to swing from the inner body, that it didn't matter what I thought as long as I could feel that way. But that line of reasoning didn't help. I said that the experience was far more important than our ideas about it, that Seamus was obviously an incredible figure whether he was mad or not.

He turned and glowered at me. "Wha' do ye mean, whether he's mad or na'?" he snarled. I could feel the blood rushing to my stomach. "Yer world is mad, young man," he spit the words at me and rose abruptly. "Let's go. This has been a mistake, I can see." His totally unexpected sensitivity had broken some unspoken code we had adopted with each other. I began pleading with him to stay and wait for Seamus, confessing my stupidity about the strange things he was showing me, my timidity, my lack of experience. I remember being on my knees through most of it looking up at him as I pleaded for another chance, like a pathetic lover. My unexpected performance must have startled him as much as his had startled me. He frowned as he looked down at me. There was a long silence as he studied my face, then suddenly he smiled. "Git off yer knees," he said, wagging his head, "ye look lik' yer askin' me to marry ye." I pleaded with him to stay and after a reflective pause he sat down again. I quickly added some branches to the fire. I was determined by now to wait all night if necessary for Seamus's appearance. Still confessing my total ignorance of things mystical and occult, I managed to get him talking about his teacher.

"Ye see the world is na' ready for someone lik' 'im, ye can see tha' from yer own reactions. The world was na' ready for Pythagoras either." The name of the Greek philosopher was intoned as if we both understood that he was one of the keys to history. He pronounced it Pith-uh-gor'-us. "The wardle was na' ready for Pith-uh-gor'-us either," he repeated the statement with a melancholy look. "Ye see Pith-uh-gor'-us had *the clue*." This was said with solemn emphasis. I was touched and amused by his quaint self-educated assurance. I had studied the pre-Socratic Greek philosophers that spring at

Stanford and knew something about Pythagoras. I wondered what the clue might be.

"Now there are some things I could tell ye, if I thought ye'd tak' 'em seriously," he went on, eying me suspiciously. I urged him to tell me, promising that all my doubts had sub-sided. "Well, I'd lik' to tell ye . . ." His voice trailed off as he studied my expression. "Well, I'll *do* it," he said quietly. "The world should o' followed the lead of Pith-uh-gor'-us." He almost whispered the words. "And 'tis this—*to ken the world from the inside*, not the outside as we've done. Like I showed ye wi' yer gowf shots there." He gestured toward the open space we had used for our practice. "Tha' is how Pith-uh-gor'-us heered the music o' the spheres—and started all our science." My mind raced back over the passages I had read about the famous philosopher. I remembered that he had invented the word "philosophy," that he had discovered certain relationships between musical intervals, that the Pythagorean theorem had been named after him, that he had founded a school in Crotona for the practice of philosophy, mathematics, and the good life.

"After Pith-uh-gor'-us science turned to magic, naethin' but superficial powers," he continued. "And so we rely upon our instruments instead o' oursel's. Tha' is why Seamus says we only need a baffin' spoon like his to play a round o' gowf—if we would e'er *ken the world from the inside.*" He stood and kicked the embers into new flame. Then he picked up Seamus's "baffing spoon" and fondled it. "Do ye ken what Seamus is really doin' heer?" he asked. "He's makin' himself into a livin' laboratory to right the balance o' our Western science, to show us how to know true gravity." He lapsed into silence, and for several minutes we stared into the fire.

"True gravity, 'tis Seamus's term for the deeper lines o' force, the deeper structure of the universe. But this is the thing," he raised his hand and shook a finger at me, "ye can only know wha' it is by livin' into it yersel'—not through squeezin' it and shovin' it the way they do in the universities and laboratories. Ye must go into the heart o' it, through yer own body and senses and livin' experience, level after level *right to the heart o' it*. Ye see, Michael, merely shootin' par is second best. Goin' for results like that leads men and cultures and entire worlds astray. But if ye do it from the inside ye get the results eventually and *everythin' else along with it*. So ye will na' see me givin' people many tips about the gowf swings lik' they do in all the 'how-to' books. I will na' do it. Ye must start from the inside, lik' I showed ye there." He pointed again to our sandy practice area. "And tha' is wha' Seamus is doin'!" He shook his head slowly. "But no one understands, and poor Seamus runs away."

He lapsed into silence once more. My memory of the conversation blurs at this point but I remember asking him about Seamus's shillelagh. I wondered if it had taken on the old wizard's presence, like the seamless robe of Christ in Lloyd Douglas's book. Of course that was just a story, I said, while this was real, but it was the same idea.

"It gave ye a good swing there, Ah could see," he said with a sly smile, "but tha' is just another kind o' magic—Seamus's magic. 'Tis no different from the magic o' science and steel-shafted clubs, just another kind. Tha' is why he will na' let me try it on the links heer. Says it's just another diversion. O' coorse, the members might na' let me use it either."

In the midst of these ruminations about Seamus MacDuff and true gravity he suddenly exclaimed (I cannot recall the exact context of the remark), "Or Western science'll run into a stalemate and then," he raised a doubled fist for emphasis, "and then thair'll be no more answers for us until we ken this world from within."

As we gazed at the dying fire a small rock-slide started down the fairway side of the ravine. We looked up into the shadows but could see nothing above us, just the rocks receding into utter darkness. "Ye know, Michael," he said, "I've of'en wondered what it'd be like to play the coorse wi' the baffin' spoon." Apparently his earlier remarks were still on his mind. "I've of'en been tempted tae do it when he's na' around." He poked a stick into the embers. Then he turned to me. "Why don't we try it now?" he said with a gleam in his eyes.

"You mean now—in the dark?" I wasn't sure if I had heard him right.

"Right now, wi' one o' the featheries." He stood as he answered and picked up the shillelagh. I asked him what would happen if we lost them.

"Tha' is what scairs me about it," he seemed to lose his zest for the idea as he considered the dire consequences of our losing Seamus's precious featheries. Research into the structure of the universe would be impeded, I imagined, if they were lost in Lucifer's Rug. But then to my utter surprise he picked up the two old balls and the club and gestured for me to follow. He walked 20 or 30 yards up the ravine, then started climbing upward toward the fairway. I stumbled along after him. We had come to a precipitous stairway carved into the cliff, with steps about a foot wide and four inches deep. He scrambled up this dangerous path like a sailor going up a rigging, holding the club and balls in one hand, and grasping the tiny ledges with his other. I inched my way after him, expecting to slide back at any moment.

It was a frightening climb. Near the top I started to look down, but thought better of it and pressed my nose to the cliff. After a five-minute climb I finally came out on level ground, back into the windy night. It was the thirteenth tee. He reached down to help me up the final steps.

"Do ye think we should do it?" he asked with an edge of doubt in his voice. "I wonder if this is a good idea."

I said that he wasn't going to get me to hit one of the balls, seeing that I was almost bound to lose it in the Rug. I could hardly breathe after the strenuous climb. "I think ye're right," he said. He was having second thoughts about the whole thing.

He walked over to the tee and put the balls on the ground. It was pitch black and the wind was still blowing, though not as hard as it had been when we arrived an hour before. You could see the silhouette of the cypress trees on the hill. The flag was lost in the darkness though, so he would have to judge where it was from the position of the trees. "What do ye think?" he asked again.

We stood there in the windy dark staring up the forbidding hill. "What would Seamus do if you lost his balls?" I asked.

"I don't know," he answered. "I don't know. It would be somethin' awful." I wondered what was compelling him to try it. "What do ye think?" he asked, almost pathetic now in his indecision.

"Do you think you could reach it, especially in this wind?" I wondered, surveying what must have been one of the world's most difficult golf holes. How he ever thought he could hit a ball made of feathers 200 yards on a windy night with an Irish shillelagh was beyond me.

"Oh, I think I can do that awright," he answered softly. "It's hittin' it straight in the wind that makes me wonder. But wha' would Seamus do if we lost his balls?"

"I'm not hitting any," I made the point again with stronger emphasis.

Apparently he hadn't heard me. "Heer," he said, "you hit first. I'll get my line from *yer* shot."

"Oh, no, not me." I backed away from the proffered club, as if it were a dangerous snake.

"Now, Michael lad"—he was suddenly composed and re-assuring—"it'll do ye a world o' good. Come try. Just one shot."

I was dumfounded at his insistence. I began to wonder if something had gone wrong with him. He must have seen that I was not going to play the hole, however. He turned abruptly and put a featherie on the tee. Then he lined up toward the invisible flag and waggled the ancient shillelagh. He waggled it slowly, and then he swung. There was a hissing sound as the ball took flight. I could not follow it, but then, above the hill, we could see where it was. It was gleaming against the sky, a luminous white point hanging like a tiny moon before it dropped toward the green.

"Aha, aha," he cried. "The old spoon did it, it did it!" He

did a little jig around the tee. I hadn't seen him so excited all day. "The old spoon did it!" he cried as he jumped and clicked his heels.

He started up the incline to the green, deciding apparently that one shot was enough, and I ran after him. Our anticipation was high as we approached the top, for we knew the ball might be lost. I had seen MacIver put a good shot into the Rug that afternoon, and there were drop-offs on all sides. We also knew that it might be very close to the pin.

But when we reached the crest of the hill there was an awful sight. Though the green was visible enough, no ball was there to be seen. Moreover, there was no pin, no flag.

"Where is the flag?" I asked. I was afraid to ask about the ball.

"Hiven knows," was the only answer he gave, in a barely audible voice. He went to the back edge of the green and peered into the darkness below. There was no ball there. I looked over the edge of the green on the ravine side.

"Maybe it fell in the gorse," I said with growing anxiety. I started back down the hill and began running my foot through the grass between the green and Lucifer's Rug.

"It's na' there," he said impatiently. "I hit it over the green if I hit it anywhere. I'll be damned," he said as if he could not believe his eyes. "I'll be damned." He whistled between his teeth, as if he could feel the impending wrath of Seamus MacDuff.

"Well, what'll we do?" I asked.

"Hiven knows," was his only answer.

I was crossing again toward the back edge of the little hill when I had a sudden idea. Then, as if I were drawn by the first flash of the premonition, I looked down as I crossed the middle of the green. There in a dark declivity, in the hidden cave of the pinless hole, lay Seamus's featherie. It was faintly luminescent as it peered at me from its dark resting place, an eye peering out of the deep.

"Shivas, here it is!" I cried and picked it up. "It's here in the hole!"

"I'll be damned," he said, his eyes more crosseyed than ever. " 'Tis the first time I e'er shot a hole-in-one on the thirteenth." He looked at the shillelagh, and kissed its mean-looking burl. "Ye saved my life, ol' spoon," he said with enormous relief. "Thank ye kindly."

We Are All Kites in That Wind

We crawled back down the rocky stairway, both of us relieved that we had come through unscathed. God knows what might have happened if that ball had been lost.

When we got to the bottom of the ravine we threw some last sticks on the fire and resumed our conversation. I think we talked mainly about English and American football, seeking respite from the strenuous adventure we had embarked upon.

The sky was turning gray now along the edge of the canyon. Summer dawn comes early in Scotland, it must have been around 2:30 or 3:00. Our fire had burned itself out and I was beginning to realize that Seamus was not to make an appearance. We both stood and stretched. Birds were singing in the cliff wall above us; they too were getting ready for the day. As the contours of the ravine gradually appeared, I could see that this was a redoubtable fortress indeed from which to conduct research subversive to the Western world. Shivas put the featherie balls and shillelagh back in their hiding place and said no to my final request to see Seamus's cave. " 'Tis as cursed to strangers as King Tut's toomb," he said. "Ye might na' survive it." He gave that abrupt decisive gesture for me to follow which he had given several times that night and we started back along the ravine floor. When we got to the rock-slide down which we had originally come he turned and looked me straight in the eye. "Michael," he said, "I want ye to do one more thing, since

I've let ye in on all these mysteries. Will ye do it?" I asked
him what it was. "I want ye tae yell lik' I do, like this . . ."
and he let out that bloodcurdling scream. I started back.

"Now just try it once," he said. I looked around the canyon,
as if someone might be watching, cleared my throat and gave
a choked little yell. It was a pathetic attempt, a constipated
bleat after his bellowing warrior cry. "Try again," he urged.
The second one was better, but I realized how deficient I was
at yelling. He wagged his head at me with a sly smile, and we
started up the rocky path.

Birds were singing in the growing light as we walked
through the damp and deserted golf links. I followed the trail
of footprints Shivas left in the grass, kicking up drops of
water and pondering these strange events. We found his car
and drove back into town. Neither of us felt like sleeping.
"Since ye dinna' have anythin' fit to drink, come to my place,"
he said and I jumped at the invitation. I was curious to see
how he lived and it would be good to get a drink of something warm or warming.

He parked where we had found his car near The Druids'
Inn and led me to the gray stone house in which he had an
apartment. We went up through a narrow staircase that was
separate from the main entrance to the house and ducked
through a tiny door into his sitting room. It was not the kind
of place I had expected, but I could see at once that it was all
his. The wooden ceiling was no more than eight feet high,
maybe less, and latticed windows stood two feet off the floor.
Shelves of books lined two of the walls and another was
covered with long sheets of brown wrapping paper, hanging
from wooden cornices near the ceiling. These paper tapestries
were covered with lists and odd diagrams. A wood-burning
stove stood in a corner near a roll-top desk; old bags of golf
clubs were stacked in another. A threadbare rug covered
most of the floor; it had a faded blue line sewn into it which
he apparently used to practice his putting alignment. It was a
small place for so large a spirit, I thought; no wonder he

spent so much time roaming the streets of Burningbush and the spaces of his inner life.

He built a fire in the iron stove and put a kettle of water on to boil. "Sit," he said, pointing to a battered leather couch that had stuffing coming out of it at some of the seams. He made a pot of powerful tea, a recipe he had learned from an officer of the Black Watch who had been a student of his, a recipe they had discovered in Afghanistan or some such place that was supposed to light up the mind. The bittersweet taste of it sent a shiver up my back. He settled into a big stuffed armchair (he called it his "meditation chair"), and turned on a creaky-looking reading lamp against the gray morning light. We sipped our mind-warming tea in silence. We were awkward with each other again, as we had been at the Inn. The compression of the little room perhaps took an edge off his freedom; it occurred to me that he always seemed more subdued indoors. As we sipped our tea he leaned back against the armchair to gaze at the ceiling. Cupping my hands for warmth around the cup, I studied the paper hanging against the wall behind me. It had lists of philosophers neatly printed in a vertical column down one side and a list of inventions printed in a column down the other. Lines connected some of the philosophers with some of the inventions. At the very top of one chart there was printed in large block letters the title DANGEROUS CONNECTIONS. Scanning the lists again, I saw that some of the connecting lines were red and some were green.

The room was getting warmer as the stove gave forth its heat. I took off my jacket and we sat sipping our tea in silence. His eyes were closed now, he seemed to be dozing or resting. I got up and tiptoed over to the bookshelves. He had gathered an impressive library, several hundred books at least. The first one my eyes settled on was a copy of *Sartor Resartus* in a long row of leather-and-gold volumes by Thomas Carlyle. Max Müller's entire *Sacred Books of the East* was there and the complete works of Coleridge. An extraordinary collection for an obscure golf professional. On one shelf a large book of photographs depicting Sam Snead's swing in all its phases was sandwiched between the *Enneads* of Plotinus and a musty old copy of the Koran.

He was still leaning back against his comfortable armchair. I took a volume that was familiar to me, *The Gospel of Sri Ramakrishna*, and sat down again on the decrepit leather couch. So many of the books he had gathered around him were familiar; it was almost the library I would like to have. I leafed through the Ramakrishna volume, a large, handsome edition containing the conversations of India's greatest nineteenth-century mystic lovingly recorded by his disciple "M." Thinking that I would visit Dakshineswar, where Ramakrishna had undergone his incredible search for God, I found some pictures of the famous temple there. As I leafed through the photographs, my head began to nod—I jerked up with a start and reached down for my cup of tea. I sipped it slowly, feeling the warmth spread out in my chest. Shivas was sitting erect now, facing away from me at an angle, I could see that his eyes were open. He stared straight ahead as if he were concentrating on something across the room. I put the cup down on the floor and continued leafing through the book. I read a page or two of Ramakrishna's sayings, marvelous passages I had read before, and looked at the pictures. I reached down for the tea and looked at Shivas again; he was still sitting erect as he stared across the room. He was absolutely motionless. I cleared my throat to catch his attention but he did not respond. There was something odd about his posture; I could feel it, something had happened. I stood up and tiptoed around in front of him—and suddenly felt faint. His eyeballs were rolled back leaving nothing but white. He was totally unconscious. I felt his pulse, my heart pounding, and bent over to smell his breath. He was still alive. Epilepsy? Heart attack? Stroke? I looked wildly around the room fighting off the first sense of panic, my mind a complete blank. Then, as if by reflex, I stumbled down the narrow staircase and knocked at the main entrance

to the house. No one answered. I knocked again more insistently, but there was still no answer. The street in front of the
house was deserted. It was still early, probably around four
o'clock, every window on the block was shuttered. I ran back
up the stairs and fumbled around the apartment looking for a
telephone book—under the desk, on the shelves, apparently
he didn't have one. I picked up the phone and dialed o, and
got a buzzing sound, then remembered that 999 was the
emergency number. A voice answered as soon as I dialed, a
man's voice. I remember how eerie it seemed having a man
answer. I told him someone was dying, glancing back at
Shivas. "I know someone who might come down," the voice
said calmly, then I could hear a clicking as connections were
made. A long moment passed while the clicking continued.
Shivas sat rigid as a corpse, his eyes rolled back, without
moving or falling forward as well he might have from his
sitting position. He couldn't have been drunk, I thought, after
everything we had been through. Still no answer on the other
end of the line. "We're having a little trouble, but hold on,"
the man's voice reassured me. Finally someone answered, an
irritable rasping old voice, "Yes, what is it?" I told him that
someone was dying. "What's he dyin' of?" the old voice
asked, intoning the word "dyin" in a kind of sing-song. I said
that I didn't know. He asked if there was some way I could
describe what was happening, some symptom, anything.
"Tell me *how* he's dyin'," the old voice rasped. I began
fumbling for words, but as I did Shivas spoke quietly behind
me. "I'm all right, Michael. Tell him I'm all right." There he
sat fixing me with those crystal blue eyes.

"Good God, you scared me," I said, then turned and apolo-
gized to the voice on the other end of the line and hung up
the receiver. At that moment I could have sworn I saw an
aura around him. For a moment he was sitting in a pool of
turquoise light—just for a second—then I could feel some
quick shutter close in my brain. He looked slowly around the
room and flexed his hands. "Have I been gone long?" he
asked quietly.

"Around fifteen minutes maybe."

"I almost disappeared," he said softly. "Almost disappeared."

"Shit, you scared me to death."

A smile began to form on his face, spreading slowly as if the muscles around his mouth had grown stiff. His eyes looked straight into mine, they were not crossed at all. "Do ye na' ken ye're flyin' heer like a kite—wi' nae mair than a threid holdin' ye?" He raised his muscular hands and snapped an imaginary string between them. "We're all kites in that wind," he said. And off he went into trance again.

For another half hour or so he sat there erect, looking like a corpse more than anything else but soaring within to regions I could only guess at. I was frightened, angry, and spellbound by turns. In the Ramakrishna book there is a picture of the saint's disciples staring up at him with bulging eyes as he stands in ecstatic trance. I must have looked like that as I watched the incredible corpse in front of me.

I closed a banging shutter and huddled at one end of the couch with my knees drawn up. I finally roused myself, stoked the fire, and made another cup of tea, circling carefully around the corpse which had grown enormous now with its mysterious presence. I sat watching him, wondering if I could ever brave the skies he was exploring. After all, that was what I was going to India for. The lamp shade glowed like an ember against the cold winds of those inner spaces, winds that could snap the thread that held me there.

But there is some inexorable density in the brain. Fear and awe gave way to sleep and my head began to sink. I was beginning to drowse, in front of the first ecstatic trance I had ever seen. I do not know how long I napped, for in sleep experience is transposed to another order of time: some barely tangible presence was entering my body, locking my joints, reassuring me—while a parade of images drifted past, memories of childhood, odd dreamlike shapes floating through the stillness of the room. His presence was entering mine by some osmosis, drawing me toward it by gentle steps.

I was cradled in a pleasurable field, held in a stillness carrying premonitions of vaster realms and tiny hints of music, music I might have heard if my brain were more open and finely tuned—distant horns, shudders of ecstatic voices just an eyelash flick away. Something in me was reaching toward those close yet distant realms but the weight of sleep pulled me back.

It was hard to tell how long it lasted. He broke the silence in a voice so faint that I thought at first I was imagining it, some words, then he cleared his throat. I looked around the room savoring the earthy familiarity of everything in it, interfused now with stillness and pleasure. " 'Tis amazin' to me how these forms, these bodies, these ideas float in this emptiness . . . strange gravity," he whispered the words in a soft hoarse voice. We looked at each other through the subtle presence that filled the room. "Just kites in that wind," he said with that bucktoothed grin and slowly stretched as he rose from his chair.

He disappeared into another room and I slowly looked around me. Everything sparkled with a new clarity as the morning brightened. I felt a freshness and pleasure as if I had slept well, and a calm poise that seemed to hold me. I was curious to know more about this amazing room.

Long brown scrolls of wrapping paper covered one entire wall. Each had a title at the top: DANGEROUS CONNECTIONS and GOD IS WAKING UP are two I remember. Another was entitled HISTORY OF THE BODY, with lists of historic events joined by red and green lines to names of political leaders, philosophers, and artists, to organs of the body including the heart, liver, kidney, and lungs, and to certain psychic centers like the Indian chakras. It was a complex chart depicting, I think, his own notions of how consciousness has unfolded in the world during historical times and how the body, or the general human awareness of the body, has developed along with it. He found me studying it when he came back into the room.

"Wha' d'ye think o' that?" he asked matter-of-factly.

"Well, I've never seen anything like it. I don't understand it really."

"Not many people have seen them, and no one yet has understood, 'sept Seamus." He had begun fixing us breakfast. As I studied the charts he fried some eggs, sliced a loaf of brown bread, and set some plates on a table near the stove. The food tasted marvelous, I felt exhilarated now. My admiration of him was growing every hour we were together. I asked him if he had ever written down his thoughts, that he should, seeing how deeply he had gone into things.

"Well, Michael, I'm against writin', seein' how many books there are in the world. It's the livin' of these things that counts. The livin' of them." Then after a long pause, "But I do have some writin's, would ye like to see them?" He looked at me bashfully. "They're funny writin's."

I said that I would be fascinated to see anything he had written. We finished eating and he cleared the table. Then he turned and regarded me with his solemn look. "Michael," he said, "I'm goin' to show ye my writin's. Yer only the third person to see them, after Seamus and Julian. Come heer." He led me into the other room. It was small and low-ceilinged with a bed and dresser and latticed windows. He stood in front of what was apparently a closet door and hesitated. Then he opened it and motioned for me to follow. It was a linen closet some ten feet deep, lined on one side with books, on the other with shelves of clothes. As I followed him into it he said gravely, "Rimember, ye must not tell anybody about this." This hidden library, this collection within a collection, seemed to center around occult lore of various kinds. Madame Blavatsky's *The Secret Doctrine* and *Isis Unveiled* were there, Bishop Leadbeater's books on the chakras, Aurobindo's *Life Divine*, and a copy of Ben Hogan's *Power Golf*! There were two or three more books about golf by authors I had never heard of. At the end of the narrow closet hung another brown chart, entitled THE BASIC STRUCTURE OF THE UNIVERSE. On it was drawn the figure of a man some three feet high, like the figures you see on anatomical charts except that it was divided into various centers and levels of consciousness instead of the usual bodily organs. Crisscrossing the entire chart were lines of psychic latitude and longitude: apparently it represented the entire human race. Behind the chart there was a small door, perhaps a laundry chute. It occurred to me that it might lead to yet another library or secret chamber.

He kneeled down and lifted a small stack of notebooks from the lowest shelf. "Heer they are," he said, looking up at me bashfully. "What d'ye think?" I said that I would have to read them before delivering any judgment. He stood and let me out, pausing once more to lift a warning finger. "Rimember, ye must na' tell anybody about this," he said.

He laid the notebooks on the table in his sitting room. They were a ragged collection, some of them obviously dating back twenty years or more. One was a ledger book with narrowly spaced writing lines, filled with what I learned was his recent handwriting. Another was a ringed binder with a yellowed label on its cover, full of handwriting that was quite different, with large looping letters, a fancier, more flowery style. His thought and expression had changed, I discovered later, from an extravagant romantic style reminiscent of Thomas Carlyle to rough, pithy sentences more like Heraclitus and the *Upanishads*. He watched me suspiciously as I leafed through the pages, scanning the titles and sayings that struck my eye. I can still remember the very first words I saw: "*Shiva* without *Shakti* is *Shava*," a gnomic phrase that turned out to be an old Hindu saying.*

"Some o' this may not make sense to ye, because they refer to my charts," he said after I had scanned all the notebooks. He seemed ill at ease, almost apologetic. "I think ye should see some other things I have, if ye're goin' to put it all

---

* Dr. Haridas Chaudhuri, of San Francisco's California Institute of Asian Studies, my authority on Sanskrit and Indian philosophy, explained that *shava* is the Sanskrit word for corpse. *Shakti* is the creative, female, time-involving, world-manifesting aspect of the Supreme Being. *Shiva* is the God of Destruction, Redemption, and Liberation.

together," he said abruptly. I had the feeling he was sorely conflicted about letting me read further.

He went over to a huge trunk standing under the brown wall-charts and opened it. As he pulled up the lid the first rays of sunlight broke through the latticed windows. I looked outside. The golden edge of sunrise framed the gray houses across the street from his study window.

"Michael, lad," he enunciated my name, "how much of our conversation have ye forgotten?" He was facing me from across the room as he stood in front of the open trunk. The question surprised me. I gave some self-effacing response, mumbled something about how vivid it was to me. "Come on, come on now," he said, his broad Scots dialect full of authority. "I can see ye dinna' ken the limits o' yer memory." I was too surprised and embarrassed at his sudden change of attitude toward me to muster a reply. Showing me his charts and notebooks had affected him, I said to myself.

"Ye see, Michael, I'm afraid ye'll forget all this," he continued. "I've learned my best students and friends forget. Or e'en worse"—he shrugged—"they rimember it wrong when I tell 'em. Sometimes I think I need to start a monastery. Which leads me round to this," he pointed down into the trunk. "But first, I must ask ye, who can teach us about rimemberin'? Think now, who can teach us?" He looked across the room at me with eyebrows raised. I said that I didn't know. "Well, I'll tell ye," he said emphatically, "the advertisers, that's who."

I was dumbfounded by this turn of the conversation. "The advertisers!" I exclaimed. "Even here in Burningbush?"

"Yes, sometimes they do it like masters," he said with a triumphant gleam. "With heraldry and pageants and cunning toorns. I've been usin' their methods."

"Their methods! Good God!"

"Some o' them have stumbled right into the first principles of occultism," he said with a look of great portent. "Put a symbol into the mind and it takes on a life of its own. Just think about it." I thought about a tune I often remembered from a television ad for Hamms Beer, and a bear beating time with its tail to a tom-tom. I had often wondered why the image was so indelible.

"Strong images are like seeds in our soul," he went on. "When they're planted there they grow, start havin' a powerful effect. Propagandists know that." I wondered who the "propagandists" were. They seemed to form a clear category in his thinking.

"But now," he said emphatically, "and this is the point, ye can make' the principle work for you. The symbols and images yer soul needs are all around ye. Tak' the hidden meanin's o' golf—a lot o' it is in those notes ye have there. I use them to remind myself." He turned and reached into the trunk. Fascinated, I moved closer. He took out a stack of picture frames and placed it on the floor, then closed the trunk. Then he carefully arranged the frames on the trunk and along the wall. "Look at these," he said as he arranged them. I can remember the images within those frames as if I had seen them yesterday.

They were all photographs, some in vivid color, some in black and white. They all had immense detail and a fine-grained clarity reminiscent of Edward Weston. The most startling thing about them was the perspective they brought to familiar places on a golf course. One showed a putting green from above, it must have been taken from a tree. At first I could not comprehend the small point in the picture's center. Then I gradually realized it was the flag and pin—the camera must have been held directly above them, directed straight down into the hole! Another, in colors shading through turquoise and green, showed a putting green and flag taken from about a foot above ground level, perhaps 25 feet from the pin. On a level with the green stood the tee, on the tee stood a player hitting his shot with a driver, apparently some 350 yards or more away. The uncanny thing about the picture again was the perspective: the player seemed exactly as tall as he would have been on the green itself. He was obviously driving toward the hole, but he already seemed to be on the green!

A third photograph showed a ball in flight about 3 feet away, coming out of the setting sun into the eye of the camera. A black ball, coming with terrific velocity! When I recall that image at times I see it exploding out of the light into my face. Sometimes when I am falling asleep the memory of it brings me awake with a start.

A fourth picture was a color portrait of Shivas himself looking directly into the camera. The immense detail of the photograph gave prominence to each pore and piece of stubble on his face. His face in fact was like a field; indeed, there was no apparent boundary between it and the brownish-green fairway around him. Then I realized the picture was a double exposure, that his own full figure appeared in his left eye, holing out a putt. The double exposure had given his face a second aspect: it was the green he was putting on!

Another picture, the most incandescent and prismatic of them all, was a high-speed shot of a golf swing, the kind you see in studies of Palmer or Snead. The remarkable thing about it was the spectrum of color and brilliant lighting. Shivas said the effect came from sunlight "through the prism of the swing." In his notes there was an obscure sentence about "a feathered body of revolving shafts, a propeller of moons, a symbol of the original emanation . . ." that possibly referred to this dazzling image.

On the floor, in the corner, as if it were hidden, stood a frame with an elaborate drawing instead of a photograph. It resembled the figure hanging at the back of his closet, a kind of medical chart depicting the human race with undecipher-able lines of psychic latitude and longitude running through it. The chief difference between it and the figure in the closet was that this Representative Man held a golf club.

There was a profound silence as we pondered this extraordinary gallery. Shivas seemed totally absorbed, as if he were seeing it all for the first time. I looked at the picture which stood on the floor directly in front of me. It had apparently been taken from within the hole itself. Through a perfectly round aperture you could see Shivas's face looking down into the camera while appearing over one rim of the circle was a golf ball, beginning its descent into the hole.

Perhaps it was the lack of sleep or the series of shocks to my ordinary frames of reference, but the pictures now began to waver; I felt an edge of nausea as one of them went completely out of focus. I lay back and looked at the ceiling, letting my attention settle on a point there. I stared at it for several minutes, and gradually felt a sense of relief. I sat up slowly. Sunlight was streaming through the latticed windows. Shivas was still gazing into the pictures, which had begun to sparkle in the slanting beams of light.

"Well, Michael, what d'ye see?" his resonant voice cut through the morning chill. He was looking straight ahead as he asked the question, at a picture he had placed on top of the chest. Holding up a hand to shield my eyes, I squinted into the brightness to see what he was looking at. And there it was. A portrait of Ben Hogan, staring directly into the camera. No double exposures, no strange perspectives, just Hogan himself, big as life!

"Well, what d'ye mak' of it?" he asked again. I could only mumble some formless reply.

For the next hour or so he seemed unsure of himself. He was showing me things he had hidden from the world, and was as uncertain about it as a struggling young writer might be about his first novel. But he grew more confident as the morning wore on, seeing that I was awed by it all. Indeed, awe is not the only word I could use. I was dumbfounded, fascinated, and finally dazed from all the blows to my usual perception. His little gallery of pictures, charts, and writings was more confounding than the *Koran* or *Finnegans Wake*.

As he grew more confident he began making more explicit hints. What he was gingerly working up to—what he had been working up to, I think, from his first invitation to visit his apartment—became more apparent. He wanted me to be some kind of link with the outside world, a Boswell, an editor, an agent, or some other role, I don't think he knew which, as long as I was a translator of any kind to the world at large.

He was shyly coaxing and prodding me to explore his work. "Why don't ye read these through," he said, arranging all the notebooks in chronological order, "and I'll get us somethin' to eat. Now come spend the day and we'll play more golf."

It was hard to resist his proposal. Though I was feeling the fatigue of our adventures, the tantalizing promise of his odd paragraphs and incredible gallery of charts drew me on. I pored over them for several hours, all that morning, through lunch, until I left that afternoon. He went out for a while to get us something to eat.

He returned an hour later in high spirits. As he put away the groceries he softly sang a lilting Irish ballad about someone named "Peter Putter" and his adventures in the wheels of time, and did a little jig around the room. He came over to me. "I'm glad ye're heer," he said, looking down at me with great warmth. "Stay the night and we'll plumb the depths o' true gravity. And who can tell, maybe we'll e'en find Seamus." He winked and squeezed my shoulder, then turned back to his groceries and started making us a meal. He seemed enormously pleased to have me there. Encouraged by his growing affection, I began asking him about his past, especially about certain events he described in his journals. And then I had the good sense to walk over to The Druids' Inn, get my camera, and photograph a letter he had just written. I even persuaded him to sit for a portrait in his meditation chair. He posed with great solemnity, eyeballs down this time. What a loss when that photograph disappeared!

He was, I discovered, half Irish and half Scottish, O'Faolin on his mother's side, born of a dour, prosperous father and a mother "who made God's eyes while she sang old Catholic hymns and bawdy songs." His parents and his birth signs, he said, had conspired to make him "a veritable saloon of conflicting impulses." Indeed, when he read in the *Religio Medici* about man the "great and true amphibian" he instantly recognized that exciting and painful truth, for he was full of urges in many directions. His teen-age years had been a torment, until the stormy events of his nineteenth summer.

He was a gifted player in his teens and members of the Burningbush club had wanted to send him to America to play on a tour, as a reminder that Scotland could still produce champions. But another destiny had been growing in him, he said. In those days he often played 45 or 54 holes of golf at a stretch through the Northern summer evenings, a kind of sensory deprivation, and while he walked those endless miles around the links strange states began to steal over him. He had an image of countless lives one day as he circled round the course and then a vastness settled in his mind, a sense which would remain with him for the rest of his life—that everything transpired in the bottomless void. (His sense that each round of golf was a new incarnation was heightened, he said, by the fact that the eighteenth green at Burningbush was built on the remains of a graveyard.) This experience had led him to philosophy and Eastern wisdom and he began to collect the books and thoughts I found in his apartment some twenty years later. He had resolved to become a priest of the church—and start a revolution of the mind. Every winter through those years he wanted to be a priest, but then summer would come again and with it all those marvelous days to walk the links and flex his skills. By August he would decide to be a golf professional.

A second conflict was developing then, around people, between "the shy one" and "the brave one" in his soul. He was often "a rabbit quiverin' under a granite face"; maybe it was the split between his mother's and his father's influence. He was a stickler for rules and proper conduct, but also a "mass of awful thoughts and perceptions about people and things in

general, thoughts I couldn't account for." These conflicts had
come to a head during his nineteenth summer, leading him
into a series of psychic upheavals.

"Tha' simmer a strange fear began creepin' into me—in
the night as I was fallin' asleep sometimes, or out on the links,
or sometimes in a crowd o' people. I began to think about
epilepsy, that maybe a fit was comin' on. The thought got
worse and worse 'til I had to do things to forget it, busy
things, or runnin' to find someone to talk to, sometimes just
whistlin' to distract myself. I was in a state as the simmer
woor on, it got to be the curse o' my life. At times I thought
it wid niver leave me, that it was burnt into my brain. Then I
read some o' those books," he gestured around the room, indicating the shelves of mysticism and philosophy, "and found
out about Ramakrishna and Plotinus and people lik' that,
how Ramakrishna passed out cold for the love o' God.
Knowin' that must have given me some courage, for one day
after 45 holes o' gowf or moor I was walkin' home and I
began to shake. The thought o' the fit and the fear was comin'
back and I started swearin' and makin' my mind busy to fight
it off. And then I rimembered the ol' mystics and the thought
came, 'go into it, go right into it.' And I did. I started
imaginin' what it would be to have a fit and then I began to
shake all over. Weird images started comin' into my mind.
Pictures o' my body breakin' tae pieces, arms and legs flyin'
apart, things like that"—he began to tremble as he recalled
that shattering experience—"and then I saw the stars above
me and felt a joy. Oh, I'll niver forget it—it was my first
journey into *the one*." He said this last in a voice so low I
could barely hear him. "Ah dinna' ken how long it lasted,
maybe ten or fifteen minutes, I really dinna' ken. But howe'er
long it was it changed my life. It was the first step in findin'
my way."

This overwhelming experience had converted him forever
away from church and school. He dropped out of the college
he was attending, and made a living by caddying and giving
occasional golf lessons. But people were a torment to him.

Like some monstrous tree his psyche was throwing enormous roots into the depths of inner experience but reaching out toward his fellows with tiny branches. When he caddied that summer he hardly talked. It became almost impossible for him to be in crowds. He was embarrassed to enter the bar or dressing rooms of the club. Then the opportunity came for him to compete in the British Amateur.

The older members at Burningbush would put up the money for his expenses. Some even wanted to send him to America for the glory of their ancient club. At times he wanted to do it. But he knew that his growing phobia about people would make competition virtually impossible, what with the crowds and dinners and awards and official ceremonies. As the summer wore on and his alienation from others became more intense he began to see the world as a vast illusion, "a play of shadows against the immensity" he had seen. During those months he saw the truth in the Indian view of the world as *maya*, pure illusion; he knew what the old mystics had meant. Why return to this brawling pit when other worlds held such promise of peace and delight? He thought of going to India to join an ashram, as I was doing, or of holing up in the Outer Hebrides, in order to live entirely in the mystic state. He had "fallen into Nirvana" and now he was tempted to stay there for the rest of his life.

(As I give this brief account of what he said I realize how inadequate it is to explain such sea-changes in his character. I would need to know more, far more, to tell the full story and to fully understand him. I know from my own experience in India that great energies come into play in the mystic life, that one needs a sturdy ego from which to explore the realms of transcendence. One needs help when navigating there, for any personal weakness may become inflated with the hidden energies of the soul. Of course, help in these areas is hard to come by, at least in the Western World, and certainly there in Burningbush in the late 1930s.)

The members became impatient as the summer wore on. They finally summoned him to a meeting in the clubhouse, in the very rooms I visited decades later, under those imposing portraits of the club's heroes and captains. He had to decide now whether to play in the tournament or not. "It was the most frightenin' thing I had ever been put to," he said as he recounted the story. "I was on the verge o' faintin' all through the meetin', thought I'd faint dead away, everything seemed so unreal. No one had e'er put me on such a spot before in my entire life, or cared so much about me, or challenged my worst weakness straight on." Then, from some depth of his soul, from some region down deep where his strange roots had grown, came the response. It was a sudden burst of uncoordinated thoughts, wild talk, some of it in the Latin he had learned in school. About the pretensions of the club and all its prejudices, about its sense of privilege and lack of religion, with ramblings about God and Demons and the Mystic State. Then he launched into the members themselves, how each of them was hiding something just like he was.

The assembled group was not prepared for such an event. This early attempt at group therapy ended in total silence. No one responded as his diatribe continued, in a kind of sing-song toward the end, "something like speaking in tongues or Baptist prayer meetings." The poor members were caught between their fondness for him and their outrage. As the rant went on they began to slip out of the room with a "whole array of looks." Only one friend remained, Julian Laing, the town's doctor and psychiatrist, who had begun to formulate his eccentric theories about mental health. They stayed up most of the night together and talked about his fears and hidden thoughts. The next day he woke to a cold demand: he would have to go around to all the members and talk to them man to man. Julian had helped him see that the only way to hold his mystic high was to do his human duty. As they talked that night they had concluded that all the "messages" were telling him to follow the destiny that was being laid out for him, not to fight it like temptation. He had the talent, the members wanted to support him, everyone who knew him sensed that he had a mighty work to do. "Let God show the way," Julian had said, "even if He uses other people."

So he began to go the rounds of all the men who had been there that night, telling them about his shyness and dishonesty and fear. Some of them listened and forgave him, some backed away, out of embarrassment or "their own shyness and dishonesty." Having made the decision to build a new life, he went those rounds with all the thoroughness he was to show in compiling his endless lists of philosophers and historic events. He began to grow a fuller self, one closer to the strong, good-humored Shivas Irons I was to meet. And then he went out to face the crowds and reporters at the British Amateur.

It was another difficult initiation. At first he thought his nervousness would disappear after his brave encounters with the members of the club. But the quivering rabbit was there as usual, "like a second self, floating right there next to all my willpower." He was given a prime starting time for the opening round, and when the moment came he was pitted against one of America's most famous players in front of the tournament's largest gallery. When he stepped out on the tee and saw the crowd lining the fairway he felt as if he were in a dream—the old fear was on him again. But then he knew that "the decision to go ahead had been made far deeper than my fears and ordinary reflexes," for without stopping to consider the consequences he began a short speech to the gallery. It was a shorter version of his speech to the members, a brief pithy sermon about fear and courage, dishonesty and true fellowship, with a brief confession of his own sins and a homily about the need for a new religion. The spectators listened attentively, many of them American tourists who apparently believed this was the Scottish custom, some of them the same poor members from Burningbush. His performance did not dispel all his fear, but at least made it possible for him to hit the ball off the tee. Walking down the fairway in the crowding gallery, he ventured a handshake or two and told a couple of jokes. By the time he addressed his second shot his strength was back.

"There's nae better way to kill a dragon," he said as he told me the story, "than to charge right up to it and shove a spear down its throat. That was the day I began to look at people's faces. I was so grateful to all that gallery. One young laddie came up to me and said that speech was the greatest thing he had e'er heard, never expected it at a gowf toornament. One old woman had tears in her eyes. O' course the toornament officials were mad as hell and there was some talk, I heard later, about kickin' me out awtigither. But they couldn't, ye see, because I won my first round from the American player and broke the course record doin' it." He made a cat's cradle with his fingers. "Me and the gallery got to be like this. They thought I was somethin' special and I knew they were rootin' for me. My drives were sailin' 10 yards longer than usual—psychic force can add 10 yards to yer drives, ye know. God bless them. I never would have made it back to the world o' people if they hadn't been so good to me—they and the members here. Their help and a few risks —what a time!" He shook his head and whistled through closed teeth. "I slew the dragon awright. With one blow. Sometimes that's the only way ye can do it."

He looked at me as he told the story, as if he were deciding whether I believed him. "D'ye want to hear what happened next?" he asked. He could see that I did. "Well, we all went out together and broke the course record, that's what we did. We went out and broke the course record. After that first drive I was feelin' all that separation *gone*. I wanted to cry, I was so relieved and free o' fear. There was nae mair fear at all. I was feelin' so good I didna' look at the ball and I hit to the rough. And then things began to happen. I hit a little wedge out to the fairway. And then I knew, Holy Jesus, that the Lord had broken through again. The ball hit a hard spot and kept bouncin', about a hundred yards, almost down to the green! Just kept bouncin' along, I couldna' believe it.

Looked like a Mexican jumpin' bean. I thought I was at one o' those old *Topper* movies where things move by themsel's. So help me God, that ball just kept goin' by itself. I knew then that somethin' was goin' on wi' that gallery. They 'wanted me to *win*.'

"Well, it went on like that," he said slowly, as if he were deciding what I was ready to hear. He studied my face. "Then everything turned to Technicolor," he said at last.

"Technicolor?"

"Technicolor, full-blown Technicolor. And I could heer the insects too." He paused again. "And music."

"Music?"

"A choir way in the distance. A great choir and drums. Some o' the gallery heard it too. They heard it awright. I could tell by the way they looked at me. That laddie who came up to me at the very beginnin', he knew what was goin' on the whole eighteen holes."

A round of golf in technicolor to the accompaniment of drums—all because he overcame his shyness! As you can see, there are enormous gaps in the story. I have often wondered how much he might have doctored his tales. If I hadn't seen Seamus's shillelagh and that fantastic gallery of charts and pictures stacked up around me, I might have thought it was all fabrication.

After the tournament he could see that golf and his inner life were one destiny. He would be a golf professional *and* a philosopher, using the game to body forth the truths he was discovering within.

Once he made the decision to accept these disparate leadings he was no longer "a chameleon on a tartan plaid" responding to every situation and impulse that came his way. He had a center, at last, albeit one that would keep unfolding. He was finally growing into the self which God had intended. For several years after that Julian Laing had helped him understand these regions of the soul, had listened to him for hours and confirmed his new resolution.

But there were still some things he did not ken. To help him understand them he needed another mentor. In August 1945, two weeks after Hiroshima, he met him.

Shivas had spent the war years on a Scottish island in the North Sea as a lookout for enemy bombers, an assignment that "fit his talent for brooding." He was on a team of four men who worked alternating three-week shifts on the island with another team. Between his tours of duty he played golf on the mainland. Those five years had confirmed his calling, for during the eighteen-hour winter nights he had perfected the contemplative part of his discipline as he watched the skies for attacking planes. The constant anticipation of enemy bombers had gradually turned into a vision that God himself would descend to earth one day. This vision possessed his mind that week in August 1945.

He was on leave in Burningbush when the meeting occurred. He had gone to pray in the old cathedral, something he had always done even after he left the church. After his prayers he walked into the adjoining burial ground, "as if he were drawn there." In front of a tomb commemorating a famous golfer stood Seamus MacDuff. Shivas had seen the old man when he was a child, going around the local course on a white Shetland pony. He was one of the great characters of the town in the twenties, a prosperous eccentric inventor, who had discovered certain engineering principles that led to the development of missiles and supersonic flight. His aloof and imperious ways endeared him to many in Burningbush and outraged others, especially because his African ancestry was so at odds with the traditions of membership in the club. He was the son of a wealthy Scottish merchant, who had made a fortune in the Africa trade, and a Voodoo priestess from the Gold Coast. His father had imagined himself a kind of Richard Burton bringing back the lore of the primitive mind, and in the course of his travels had met the clairvoyantly gifted black woman who eventually gave birth to Seamus. The youngster had been raised in his mother's tribe, and tutored in British ways by teachers his father sent to the Gold Coast. He was then sent to Oxford when he was seventeen. His eventual fascination with the dark underside of modern science undoubtedly derived from his African roots. He sometimes compared himself to Amenhotep the Fourth, the monotheistic Pharaoh known as Ikhnaton, who was also a combination of Northern and Southern genes. In any case, Seamus's swarthy face and white bristling beard confounded many of the people of Burningbush who had never seen anyone like him. His habit of riding around the links on a Shetland pony only heightened the impact of his startling presence.

He had gone into seclusion sometime before 1930, no one knew why. Some thought he was mad; others said he had gone bankrupt while developing a new scheme for harnessing power.

Now he stood gazing at the statue as Shivas approached. Without turning, he said, "You and I have much to do, for these are our final days." If I correctly remember Shivas's account, their collaboration started immediately, Seamus following his new protégé around the Burningbush links as they had their first seminar on true gravity.

In the years that followed, they worked on the relations between consciousness and physical laws, Seamus being the theorist and Shivas his practitioner in the world of golf. He hinted that the old wizard had other areas in which he was trying his theories, that many other human activities would be transformed one day in the knowledge of true gravity and the "luminous body."

Hiroshima was the beginning of the end, according to Seamus MacDuff; it was the final sign that man must discover the secrets of his soul or go the way of dying species. The discovery of atomic weapons had come too soon, before the deeper revelations of science that were ultimately meant to be. Evolution had taken an awful turn and there was not much time to right the balance. He was studying the golfer's tomb that day in the cathedral burial ground because he and

Shivas had to make golf a matter of life and death. It was an appropriate place for them to meet.

Shivas Irons and Seamus MacDuff, what a pair! I don't know if I will ever live down the fact that I ran away from their incredible world.

That afternoon I abruptly decided to return to London. I have always been a sucker for exact schedules; a psychoanalyst once said I had a "completion complex." The afternoon was slipping away and the time for my train approached. Shivas had never said I should stay. He had only hinted and held out tiny blandishments. We had never really discussed what I was going to do with all the notes I was making. I had come a long way and had made elaborate plans for the trip. I had a ride to Dover and Calais from London, with a young lady I had met on the *Île de France*. I had planned my trip to India for over a year. All of this propelled me onward. At about 3:30 I said I was going to leave.

He stood and looked out a window. Then he turned and gave me a withering look that said I was unworthy of everything he had shown me. I hurriedly gathered up my notes and asked him to come with me to my room and then to the train. He reluctantly consented, and we walked over to The Druids' Inn in silence—two awkward figures, one embarrassed and nervous, the other smoldering with unspoken thoughts. I cannot remember what we said to each other then, just the feeling of it.

I can still see him waving as my train pulled away from the station, an angry figure growing smaller against the shimmering perspective of that marvelous little town.

What is repression? How does it work so insidiously in our lives? Why can't I recall what was going through my mind as I raced away from Burningbush? I only remember consoling myself during the trip to London that most of his other students must have done what I was doing.

Epilogue

But the story did not quite end there (indeed in many re-spects it is not over yet). During the following week a re-markable incident occurred in the cathedral of Rheims, one which seemed related to my adventures in Burningbush.

In London I met my companion of the *Île de France*, who was surrendering herself to the surprises of a European summer. She had rented a Morris Minor and was a jaunty chauffeur for a merry ride to Canterbury. We had not been together for more than fifteen minutes before I began to relate my story of the previous two days. Perhaps it was the shock of those events to my nervous system or the lack of sleep but I told the story in two or three different versions. Her woman's eye for the absurd and her general good spirits cast a warm spell around me and I began to sort out the deceptive complexity of that brief visit to Scotland.

While she drove, I fell into a reverie. Pleasant and seem-ingly random thoughts softened by the green English coun-tryside, then vivid scenes from my past forming and reform-ing, sorting themselves out, leading me back to childhood like hypnotic regression. I was in warm, unaccountable spirits, anticipation spreading in my cells as if I knew this reverie would bring some marvelous secret. Both of us felt that sense of zero gravity that comes when you are traveling with-out an immediate or particular goal. In Canterbury we got into the old cathedral sometime after midnight because the wizened caretaker liked the gleam emanating from this loosening of my brain.

The next day we drove to Dover and crossed the channel to Calais. I still remember the smell of a store there, a smell that was familiar at once for it was the one I grew up with in my grandparents' laundry and kitchen—salamis and parsleys and spices and consommés, a combination of ingredients I could never forget. The store in Calais brought memories of vacations in San Francisco when I was a child, with my fun-loving, pleasure-loving Grand'mère and Grand'père and all their children and cousins (many of them gourmet cooks); a peasant world, a breath of air from the Pyrenees, full of the very same smells I found in this store in Calais. These smells from the past gave body to my reverie as we drove toward Rheims, absorbing me all that day until we arrived at the great cathedral and I saw the banner and figure of Saint Jeanne d'Arc.

The memories began in earliest infancy, feelings with no graspable image or event to hold them: feelings of cradling and rocking and my mother's pleasure, a time of membranes' sensuous stretching, with textures of reassuring blankets and diapers like warm water-beds, adventures of water and air, a trip well begun; then an image of a kindergarten class, watching all the others on the merry-go-round but too uneasy to get on myself, the shy one standing near the teacher while most of the kids screamed and laughed and fell on the whirling frame; and a third-grade teacher with a wall of bugs and spiders in bottles filled with formaldehyde, my peering through protective glass at those mysterious many-legged creepy-crawlies, knowing at once what they felt like and curious thereafter about other beings, teeming worlds of them appearing in books I could find on my parents' shelves and in fortunate classrooms; then books about stars and planets and finally the mystery underlying. I became an early philosopher—late into puberty, early into God—wandering into bookstores and feeling my way to the right shelf, the opening in the mystery: somewhere in that store was a word,

it never failed, I would tell my friends that I could dowse for
books, for the Word—the trip began into those reachings of
the mind when I was still five feet four. And then the
memory of that shattering day in a class I came to by mistake, the class of Frederic Spiegelberg, known to many of the
students in those nonphilosophical nonapocalyptic days of
1950 as the best teacher on the Stanford campus, remembered him rolling the Sanskrit words, intoning the *Brahman*
and the Vedic Hymns and knowing that I could never be the
same again, that all the dowsing for books in my teen-age
years was coming into focus—at Stanford, the fun-loving
school, Spiegelberg rolling out the Vedic Hymns, bringing a
few of us home to the beginning of things; and then our little
group of dropouts in 1951, led by Walter Page, older than we
with his streak of white hair running Mohawk-style down the
middle of his head; Walt Page and his closet full of books—a
forerunner of Shivas Irons. The memory of all my teachers
and conversions rolled through me that sunny summer day
in 1956.

We drove into Rheims and circled round the great cathedral, viewing it first from our car before we found our room. I
had read a long shelf of history books before this trip, for I had
decided to recapitulate the march of Western History on my
way to India: I wanted to get my bearings, perhaps, on my
way out to sea. The cathedral of Rheims and the armor of
Jeanne d'Arc were special places on that journey back. I had
read Shaw's play and preface and two or three books about
her, for her life was one of those intersections I needed to
comprehend if I was going to find the link between this
world and the ones I was about to explore. She was a *pitha*,
as the Indians say, a place where something breaks into our
workaday world and bothers us forevermore with the hints it
gives.

We found the small hotel we had heard about and asked
for a room. Then I caused a scene by asking for *two* rooms.
My companion, first of several good women confounded by

sudden turnings of the erratic compass needle of asceticism and sensuality in my soul, was angry and hurt, and the innkeeper—well, I had never encountered one so jealous of his rooms; he thought I had asked for another because I didn't like the one we saw first, so came like a gallant Frenchman to my companion's defense. After much argument he said that this was the very last room in his inn, that, moreover, there was not another left in the entire town. So I said we would go on to Paris that night. In spite of all the trouble I was making, I had to make the renunciation, there was no resisting it; I had to prepare for whatever was emerging in these days of reverie and catharsis.

Jeanne d'Arc. I remembered seeing sailors from a French warship with her name on their caps while I was stationed in Puerto Rico, remembered my uncle's joke about being captain of the ship since he had been aboard it once in San Francisco; he had joked about it during every party at the Frenchmen's gatherings when I was a child, never tired of getting us to salute, my brother and I and all our cousins, whenever he announced he was "Captain Pierre" of the French fleet, captain of the *Jeanne d'Arc*.* As we walked toward the Gothic spires looming now above the town I remembered these and other associations to her name, an arc joining this world to the others, the charts on Shivas's wall with lines joining vertical columns, one entitled DANGEROUS CONNNECTIONS, another GOD IS WAKING UP, and his notion that God gives us a million clues but because we are so dense he must shove some of them right in our face.

Then we came to the cathedral façade. There was con-

---

* I have only to turn my head as I write to see the *Jeanne d'Arc* moored at a pier on the San Francisco waterfront.

I wrote this epilogue in Big Sur (in the spring of 1971) and returned to find a ship glowing in the water beneath me like an illuminated cathedral. At first I did not know its name. Then an announcement came over a local radio station that the *Jeanne d'Arc* was receiving visitors at pier 39—the pier beneath my window! I focused my binoculars on it, and there were the words spelled on its bow; there was no mistaking them. As a friend remarked, my ship had come in.

struction under way inside and you could see at once that much of it was newly built. The ravages of bombardment during the war were still being repaired, we were told, that was why this rear part of the towering nave looked so clean, so free of soot and all the centuries' calefactions, almost as if it had shed a skin. It was not at all as I had anticipated it, not dark and libidinous and full of mystery; it reminded me in fact of a gigantic bower, full of springtime leaves and sunbeams streaming through the unstained glass. On all sides there bustled children from some French school, whispering and giggling as they scampered after their brisk and upright teachers: their chirping voices echoed off the tall, empty windows and airy vaults, receding into waves of formless sound and the beginnings of music. The cathedral of Rheims was for all the world like an airy bower, its power and mystery was in the sound it gave back.

The sound. I was struck by the amazing swirl of it through the towering vaults: giggling children, hollow footsteps, the occasional shout of a workman rising above a quiet roar like distant surf.

The sound and then the tiny figure at the end of the nave. For there she was as I had hoped, the figure of the Maid in the original armor, carrying a banner of white that seemed four times her size.

I circled away from my friend and walked alone toward the statue, poised at last on insight's very edge. Memories recalled and impulses cleansed, mind empty now, a pious bore to my friend but ready nevertheless for the omens, I came like a sleepwalker to the point of intersections embodied in the relics of Saint Joan.

Then the omens began.

As I walked up the side aisle on the right, a weathered old lady dressed in black rose from her prayers near the aisle and watched me intently. As I passed her she grabbed my arm. Her face had a simian look, with flaring nostrils and flat high cheeks, and her eyes showed white as if they were rolled back permanently from so much prayer. *"Entendez vous les voix sous les voûtes?*" she asked with an urgent voice—did I hear the voices in the vaults? She rolled back her eyes and looked toward the cathedral roof, then repeated the question. I started to pull away but felt drawn to her strangely importuning look, for a moment I was going two ways at once.

She asked the question again with growing agitation —did I hear the voices? What was she driving at? She was mad, I thought, an eccentric old peasant woman centering her delusions in her prayers. But I followed her gestures and looked up into the cathedral vault. As I did, the echoes of the place engulfed me.

Distant ocean waves, elusive whispers were forming in the sibilant echoes. Yes, I could hear them, I could hear the voices. I sat down next to her and listened. The memories and catharsis of the last few days had prepared me perhaps for this unlikely event. I looked into the Gothic arches, up into the overturned keel of the nave. What were they saying? What were the old lady's voices saying? If I let some door in my brain swing open, there would be a voice and a word, I had learned how to do that during long hours of meditation. There was a resistance though, for the voice invariably left me with nausea—something was threatened by such interventions and reacted with an automatic visceral no. But now I was in a mood to let it come, the last few days had given me a taste for abandon, yes, whatever had begun at Burningbush was carrying me to this cathedral bench. I closed my eyes, let the swirl of sound congeal round that elusive door in my head, and sure enough the arches spoke. A tiny voice coming as if through distant echo chambers said, "Come home"—"Come home," it said again and then like distant choirs came the beginnings of music, emblazoning those words on my brain forever. Come home, come home, I was breaking through to another realm: come home, it said, follow the music home at last.

I will never know what happened next, for when I opened my eyes the old lady was gone and in her stead there sat my companion of recent days. I stretched my arms and reached out to touch her. Her hair in the sunlight was like a halo and her eyes and mouth curled upward with fond amusement. We looked at each other for a moment and I could see that she understood something of what I had seen. She leaned toward me and kissed my cheek and whispered that she would meet me outside when I was ready, then rose with a little wave and slipped away.

Perhaps an hour or two had passed, judging from the change of light. It seemed to be late afternoon and there was a hush in the cathedral now. The armor on Saint Joan's statue caught a ray of sunshine and flashed it back down the lengthening nave—perhaps the Maid was sending me signals. I felt a faint impulse to rise and explore the place, but the afterglow of trance held me in its blissful field: in the heavy stillness there was the subtlest suggestion of the fairy dust Shivas had mentioned filtering through the membranes of the inner body, as if my ordinary frame were being transformed by the explosion of light and sound triggered by the strange old lady. I sat for several minutes savoring the quiet and the process of change going on inside me and thought again of Shivas. This was the kind of thing he was into—what a pleasure and what a privilege! The thought occurred that he had passed the secret of it on to me. For it was said in most of the ancient books that *darshan*, as the Indians called it, the passing of the light, could only come directly from teacher to student, that it was rarely mediated in any other way. I said a little prayer of thanks to my Scottish golfing teacher.

The beams of light shaped by the tapering walls of glass were softening now and casting longer shadows among the branches and spreading trees on the walls of the church. I looked around the enormous space, at Saint Joan, at the people filing out the great rear doors, at the figures kneeling in prayer, then up to the Gothic columns, and the catwalks high above. High in the shadows of the nave, some 90 or 100 feet above me, a tiny figure was looking down, perhaps a workman looking for his helper. As I watched him I realized he wasn't moving, that he was looking in my direction. I could not discern his features but could see he was dressed in black with a frizzy beard, that he seemed to have a smile on his face, a mad, gay little smile.

I looked around the nave, then up at the ceiling again: the bearded face was staring down at me still, with the same little smile.

The relentless scrutiny of the distant figure was obscene. I stood up and started down the aisle toward the cathedral sanctuary to get another angle from which to see him. His head turned to follow my movement. There was no doubt about it, he was watching me intently. An old lady was sweeping at the edge of the choir; I pointed toward the figure in the rafters and asked her who it was. She shrugged her shoulders and said she did not speak English. *"Qui est-ce?"* I asked insistently, pointing again at the peering face. *"Mais de qui parlez vous? Je ne vois rien,"* she said in a rasping voice as she looked toward the distant ceiling, "I don't understand."

I jabbed my finger at the smiling face. "There, right there, don't you see it?"

"I don't understand," she answered with a shrug and turned back to her sweeping.

For a moment the lights grew dim. I looked for someone to help me, but there was no one else in this part of the cathedral. Then I noticed a figure walking toward me up the center aisle, a tall man with a dark beard and priestly suit of black, a rabbi perhaps. He seemed to be looking at the figure of Saint Joan, for as he approached his head turned slowly to keep the statue in sight. As he passed I cleared my throat and touched his arm.

"Excuse me, sir, but would you do me a favor?" As I asked the question I glanced up to check on the figure above. It was in exactly the same position, peering down at me with a clearly discernible smile.

"Yes?" the stranger paused and looked at me with a kind and curious expression. He seemed strangely familiar.

"Forgive me for this," I asked, "but I think someone is

watching me from the roof. Would you please see if you can see him?"

The stranger in black smiled through his bushy beard with a wide, slightly bucktoothed smile and said in what seemed to be a British accent, "I don't think one can get into those arches."

"But look, would you please look?" I asked again, an edge of pleading in my voice now.

"Well, then, show me where he is," he said and turned to follow my pointing finger. "I don't think there is anyone there," he said after he had scanned the long sweep of arches in the cathedral vault.

"But look, look there," I insisted, holding my arm so he could look down the line of my finger. I could see the face as clearly as ever.

"I'm sorry, I'm very sorry," he turned to face me. "I simply cannot see him. Perhaps you've mistaken a gargoyle for a living face." He smiled another bucktoothed smile and put an arm around my shoulder. "Young man," he said, "let me show you the banner of Saint Joan. That is far more interesting than a face in the roof."

I glanced again at the staring figure. But I followed the stranger, for his presence reassured me.

He led me to the base of the little statue. I could see when we got there that the Maid must have been less than five feet tall. We stood looking up at her in silence for several moments, then the kindly man in black said in his British accent, "That banner, have you ever seen it before?" I said that I had read about it and had seen it on a postcard. It was surprisingly long and I wondered how the little woman could have carried it; she must have been as strong as an ox. The stranger moved closer and reached over to touch it. Then he stroked it gently and brushed some dust from a fleur-de-lis. "She designed it herself, you know," he said. "Can you imagine the inspiration it must have been?" I was touched by his fond regard for the ancient object. My upset was going away. "Do you think it has some power still?" he murmured, almost as if he were asking himself the question. "I would love to pick it up." He touched the dusty banner now with both his hands, and for a moment I thought he might take it from the statue. I had an image of him holding it above his head and marching around the cathedral. He must have sensed what I was thinking for he turned to me and winked and said, "You be the Dauphin and I'll be the Maid." I was at ease by now and gave a little laugh. Then he smiled through his bushy beard.

The bells were tolling in the cathedral of Rheims and acolytes were lighting candles. It was time for Mass.

"Would you like to join me for the service here?" my new friend asked with an engaging smile. "Then I will tell you some secrets about Jeanne d'Arc." I was about to say yes, but at that very moment I saw him looking skeptically over my shoulder—I remember his look so well. Then I felt a hand on my neck and knew it was Dulce, my good companion come after these many hours to get me. There she was with her golden hair and twinkling eyes, patient to the end with all my dallyings.

"I'm sorry," I said to the stranger, "but we have to drive to Paris tonight. There's not a room left in Rheims."

He seemed to be disappointed. "Well," he said, with a gesture toward the cathedral roof, "at least we got rid of the ghost." I looked up and indeed the figure was gone. "I do that sometimes, see faces like that," my embarrassment must have been plain. "Thanks for your time."

I reached out to shake his hand and he gave me a bone-crunching grip. Then he smiled his bucktoothed smile for the last time and I saw that his gaze was ever so slightly crossed.

"Whenever you feel oppressed," he said, "remember Saint Joan and her angels and remember that she made herself a banner." He raised a large hand in farewell and waved it in front of his face as if he were opening and closing some invisible curtain. We waved good-by, then arm in arm we walked outside into the light of the setting sun.

PART II

The Game's Hidden
but Accessible Meaning

Certain events may reflect the significant dimensions of all
your life, mirroring your entire history in a passing moment.
Have you ever had an experience like that? Have you been
caught by an event that suddenly pulled the curtains back?
Shivas Irons maintained that a round of golf sometimes took
on that special power.

The archetypes of golf are amazingly varied, he said, that
is the reason so many people gravitate to the game.

Golf as a Journey

"A round of golf," he said in his journal notes, "partakes of
the journey, and the journey is one of the central myths and
signs of Western Man. It is built into his thoughts and dreams,
into his genetic code. The Exodus, the Ascension, the Odyssey,
the Crusades, the pilgrimages of Europe and the Voyage of
Columbus, Magellan's Circumnavigation of the Globe, the
Discovery of Evolution and the March of Time, getting
ahead and the ladder of perfection, the exploration of space
and the Inner Trip: from the beginning our Western World
has been on the move. We tend to see everything as part of
the journey. But other men have not been so concerned to get
somewhere else—take the Hindus with their endless cycles of

time or the Chinese Tao. Getting somewhere else is not nec-
essarily central to the human condition."

Perhaps we are so restless because like Moses we can never
make it to the promised land. We tell ourselves that It is just
over the next hill: just a little more time or a little more
money or a little more struggle will get us there; ". . . even
our theology depends upon that Final Day, that Eschaton
when the journey will finally arrive, to compel our belief in
God."

The symbol of the journey reflects our state, for man is
surely on the move toward something. Many of us sense that
our human race is on a tightrope, that we must keep moving
or fall into the abyss. "This world is for dyin'," he said that
night. We must die to the old or pay more and more for
remaining where we are.

Yes, there is no escaping the long march of our lives: that
is part of the reason people re-enact it again and again on the
golf course, my golfing teacher said. They are working out
something built into their genes.

But there are other myths to govern our lives, other impulses lurking in our soul, "myths of arrival with our myths of
the journey, something to tell us we are the target as well as
the arrow."

So Shivas Irons would have us learn to enjoy what *is*
while seeking our treasure of tomorrow. And—you might have
guessed it—a round of golf is good for that, " . . . because if it
is a journey, it is also a *round*: it always leads back to the
place you started from . . . golf is always a trip back to the
first tee, the more you play the more you realize you are
staying where you are." By playing golf, he said, "you re-
enact that secret of the journey. You may even get to enjoy
it."*

---

* I have often thought that his sense of golf as the journey-round
was deepened by his memory that the eighteenth green at Burningbush was built on a grave.

The Whiteness of the Ball

What the golf ball was to Shivas has been hinted; what it has come to mean for me remains unsaid. And for a reason. Its power as a symbol is so complex and labyrinthine, so capable of lending itself to the psyche of each and every player, that once an attempt like this has begun to comprehend its "inner meaning," all bearings may be lost. For the golf ball is "an icon of Man the Multiple Amphibian, a smaller waffled version of the crystal ball, a mirror for the inner body; it is a lodestone, an old stone to polarize your psyche with." The more I ponder its ramifications the more I see that each and every bit of this world reflects the whole.

A friend of mine sees it as a satellite revolving around our higher self, thus forming a tiny universe for us to govern—a marvelous image really when you think about it, one I am sure Shivas Irons and Seamus MacDuff would have approved of. Our relation to the ball is like the Highest Self's relation to all its instruments and powers; the paths of its orbits reflect those of the planets and suns. The ball is then a symbol of all our revolving parts, be they mental or physical; for a while we re-enact the primal act of all creation: the One casting worlds in all directions for its extension and delight. Shivas anticipated the image in his notes: "For a while on the links we can lord it over our tiny solar system and pretend we are God: no wonder then that we suffer so deeply when our planet goes astray."

The ball is also a reflection, as Adam Greene said, of projectiles past and future, a reminder of our hunting history and our future powers of astral flight. We can then ponder the relation between projectile and planet, our being as hunter and our being as God; the hunter, the golfer, the astronaut, the yogi, and God all lined up in the symbol of the ball.

"The ball is ubiquitous," say the notes. "It is in flight at this very moment above every continent. Moreover, it is in flight every moment of the day and night. It may take flight one day on the moon, especially when you consider the potential prodigies of mile-long drives and the wonder they would bring to millions. Consider the symbolism inherent in that indubitable fact: a golf ball suspended in air at every moment!" There are so many golfers around the globe.

At rest, it is "like an egg, laid by man," for who can tell what prodigies the next shot will bring? In flight it brings that peculiar suspended pleasure which lies at the heart of the game; it is "a signal that we can fly—and the farther the better!"—it is a symbol of our spirit's flight to the goal. It is perfectly round, for centuries of human ingenuity and labor have made it so, and "the meanings of roundness are easy to see." (Parmenides and other Greek philosophers said that Being itself was a globe, that we must therefore "circulate" our words in order to tell a "round truth.")

So the symbols and meanings are endless. But when all these are said and done, there is a fact about the ball that overpowers all the rest. It is the whiteness of the ball that disturbs me more than anything else. "Though in many natural objects whiteness enhances beauty, as if imparting some special virtue of its own," said Herman Melville in a well-known passage, "and though certain nations have in some way recognized a certain pre-eminence to it, there yet lurks an elusive something in the color which strikes panic to the soul."

Only black so reminds us of the great unknown. Black and white, we throw them together in the old cliché, but somewhere deep in both there lies a hint of powers unforeseen. Do they remind us of the void, since they represent the absence of all ordinary hue? Is it annihilation we fear when we encounter them? "All colors taken together congeal to whiteness, the greatest part of space is black," say the journal notes. "What would happen if someone introduced a golf ball painted black?"

The Mystery of the Hole

In no other game is the ratio of playing field to goal so large. (Think of soccer, American football, lacrosse, basketball, billiards, bowling.) We are spread wide as we play, then brought to a tiny place.

The target then leads into the ground, leads underground. I realized this once reaching into one of the exceptionally deep holes our Salinas greenkeeper was cutting in 1949 (he had procured a new hole-cutter). What a strange sensation reaching so far into the ground. What was down there, underneath the ball?

There was a section in his notes entitled "The Psychology of Passageways," which has a bearing on the hole's mystery. In it there was a list of "holes and doorways in our ordinary life," which included a long paragraph about the significance of looking through windows (something to the effect that windows have a function other than letting us look outside, that we build them to simulate our essentially imprisoned state), another on the subject of toilets and the draining away of our refuse (including some sentences about the need to examine our stool whenever we feel disjointed), an essay on picture frames and other boundaries on art objects, and a list of all the "significant openings" in his own apartment (apparently, he had taken a careful inventory of these). There was also a list of "Extraordinary Openings." This included a constellation in the new zodiac he had made (see "A Golfer's Zodiac," p. 153), various kinds of mystical experience—an entire catalogue in fact of transports and ecstasies; a list of historic figures (including Joan of Arc, Pythagoras, Sri Ramakrishna, Seamus MacDuff, the Egyptian Pharaoh Ikhnaton, and a Dundee cobbler named Typhus Magee); a list of historic events (including the outbreak of philosophy all over the world during the sixth century B.C., the first flights at Kitty Hawk, and a drive he had hit sometime during the summer of

1948); certain places in Burningbush and its environs (I think he compared these to the points on the body which are probed during treatments with acupuncture), a golf course in Peru (perhaps the Tuctu golf course, which he had mentioned during our conversation at the McNaughtons); certain phrases, philosophical terms, and lines of poetry (including the word *Atman*, the *Isha Upanishad*, and a limerick by one of his pupils); a list of coincidences in his life; and the unpublished manuscript of his teacher.

Our first passageways, he said, are the avenues of sense—our eyes, ears, nostrils, and mouth. We build our houses and churches to simulate these, we relate to the earth itself as if it were our body, for "we start as someone looking out, and as soon as we look we think of escape."

"Life is a long obsession with passageways," the notes go on, "we are ever breaking through to the other side—of ignorance, isolation, imprisonment. Memory, catharsis, travel, discovery, ecstasy are all ways of getting outside our original skin."

He thought it significant that an entire fairway, with its green, rough, hazards, and traps was called a "hole," that the tiny target was used to characterize all the rest of the playing field. " 'How many holes have you played?' is the way the question is asked, not 'how many fairways?' or 'how many tees?' " He thought it had something to do with the fact that after all our adventures, all our trials and triumphs on the journey-round we are left with that final passage through; that the hole and what it leads to is really what the game is all about.

As it turns out some of the most original thinking on the subject has been done by Jean-Paul Sartre, who ends Part Four of *Being and Nothingness* with a short essay on the hole and its implications. I don't recall Shivas quoting Sartre but their thinking on the subject has some extraordinary similarities. The French philosopher, admittedly, is not an accomplished golfer, but his apparent grasp of the hole's mystery suggests that he has had his problems and triumphs on the

links. "Thus to plug up a hole," he says, "means originally to
make a sacrifice of my body in order that the plenitude of
being may exist." (How we golfers can sympathize with
that.) "Here at its origin we grasp one of the most fundamental tendencies of human reality—the tendency to fill. . . .
A good part of our life is passed in plugging up holes, in
filling empty places, in realizing and symbolically establishing
a plenitude." In establishing a plenitude! Perhaps this is the
most fundamental clue. And the comprehension of that essential act of sacrifice involved in every disappearance of the ball
into the hole (sacrifice and inevitable rebirth)! For the journal notes say, "In golf we throw ourselves away and find
ourselves again and again. . . . A ball is in flight somewhere at
every moment. . . ." What are all these but glimpses of plenitude! To fill the hole with our ball is to reaffirm that fullness.

Replacing the Divot

Our green-loving philosopher claimed there was no better
way to deal with our existential guilt than replacing a divot
or repairing a friendship. "We act on friendship every moment: with our fellows, our land, our tools, with the unseen
spirits and the Lord whose world we are tending."

"Golf is a game of blows and weapons. In order that the
game continue we must make amends for every single act of
destruction. In a golf club everyone knows the player who
does not replace his divot. One can guess how he leads the
rest of his life."

Replacing the divot is "an exercise for the public good." It
is also a reminder that "we are all one golfer." There would
simply be no game if every golfer turned his back on the
damage he did.

A Game for the Multiple Amphibian

Bobby Jones and other lovers of the game have attributed its
widespread appeal to the fact that it reflects so much of the

human situation: comedy, tragedy, hard work, and miracle; the agony and the ecstasy. There is something in it for almost everyone. Shivas liked to quote the *Religio Medici*, especially the passage that described man as ". . . that great and true Amphibian whose nature is disposed to live, not only like other creatures in divers elements, but in divided and distinguished worlds." He believed that golf was uniquely suited to our multiple amphibious nature. It gives us a chance to exercise so many physical skills and so many aspects of our mind and character.

I need not catalogue the game's complexity to make my point: you know about all the long and the short shots; all the nuance of weather, air, and grass; all the emotion and vast resolution; all the schemes for success and delusions of grandeur, and the tall tales unnumbered; the trials of patience and fiendish frustrations; all the suicidal thoughts and glimpses of the Millennium. We all have a golfing friend we have had to nurse past a possible breakdown or listen to patiently while he expounded his latest theory of the game. How often have we seen a round go from an episode out of the Three Stooges to the agonies of King Lear—perhaps in the space of one hole! I will never forget a friend who declared after his tee shot that he wanted to kill himself but when the hole was finished said with total sincerity that he had never been so happy in his entire life. No other game is more capable of evoking a person's total commitment.*

This immense complexity delighted Shivas. In fact, he would add more complexity to the game, perhaps to satisfy his endlessly adventurous spirit. Running, for example, has been left out, as well as jumping and shouting; so he advocated your exercising these basic functions sometime during the golfing day if you wanted to balance your mind and nerves. We must give these large needs adequate expression, he said, otherwise golf would "imprint too much of its neces-

---

* An insightful book in this regard is *The Mystery of Golf*, by Arnold Haultain, recently reprinted by The Serendipity Press, though out of print now (ca. 1971).

sarily limited nature on us." For ". . . every game must have
its limits, simply to exist, just as every form and every culture
does, but our bodies and our spirits suffer." So somewhere
and somehow we should run and jump and sing and shout. (I
don't want to give you any advice about this, especially when
I think about some of the trouble I have had on golf courses
when I have tried to follow his advice. Perhaps you should
confine these more strenuous activities to your local school-
yard or gym. But you might find it interesting to see how
your game fares when you exercise those muscles and functions that golf neglects.)

This is true for much more than running, jumping, and
shouting though. For our golfing teacher maintained in his
inexorable way that our "emotional and mental body" needed
as much exercise as our physical body did. So "poetry, music,
drama, prayer, and love" were essential to the game too.
"There is no end to it," he said, "once you begin to take golf
seriously."

Of a Golf Shot on the Moon

It can now be argued that golf was the first human game
played on another planetary body. Those two shots Alan
Shepard hit with a six iron at the "Fra Mauro Country Club"
have brought a certain stature and gleam of the eye to golfers
the world over. Coming as they did while I was writing this
book, they appeared to me as synchronicity: the game has a
mighty destiny, the event said; Shivas Irons was right. In the
shock I felt when the news appeared (I had not seen the
television show) I thought that in some inexplicable way
those shots had been engineered by Shivas (from his worldly
hiding place) or by Seamus MacDuff (from his hiding place
on the other side). But the subsequent news that Shepard
and his golf pro, Jack Harden, had planned the thing ruled
out Shivas and restored some perspective to my hopeful speculations. Still, the meaning of it continued to loom before me.

Golf on the moon! And the command module named Kitty Hawk! (Shivas had called Kitty Hawk an "extraordinary opening" in this unfolding world and had worked with Seamus all those years on the possibilities of flight with "the luminous body.") The event was a tangle of synchronicities.

I wonder how many other golfers have felt the same way. So many of us are alive to the other edge of possibility (perhaps because the game has tried us so sorely) and ever alert for the cosmic meaning. This event confirms our sense of mighty things ahead.

There are other implications, however, some less promising. A trusted friend of mine, someone with a quick keen eye for injustice and intrigue, saw an ugly side to the whole affair. It was, he said, an imperial Wasp statement, however unconscious, that this here moon is our little old country club for whites, thank you, and here goes a golf shot to prove it. I hated to hear that, for I wanted to dwell on the hopeful meanings. And I hated to think what Seamus would do, being half-black, if he were fiddling around with it all from his powerful vantage point. The Kitty Hawk might not make it back to earth! But the heroes are back and so far so good. Still, I am left wondering what latent imperialism lay behind that six-iron shot.

And I am left with other thoughts about the character of Alan Shepard. What could have led the man to design that faulty club, smuggle it on board with those "heat-resistant" balls and risk some billion-dollar disaster from flying divots or tears in his space suit? What could have led him to such monumental triviality amid the terrors and marvels of the Moon? The madness of the game had surfaced again, I thought, as I pondered his motives.

Had NASA put him up to it for public relations reasons? Maybe they wanted some humor in the enterprise or the backing of certain rich and powerful golfing senators. Perhaps he would collect on some stupendous bet (after all, he was interested in money and had made a pile in his astronaut years). Or could it simply be that all his golfer's passion to hit the ball a mile now had a chance to express itself, indeed the chance of a lifetime, the chance of history! Perhaps the collective unconscious of all the golfing world was delivering itself at last, seizing him as instrument for the release of a million foiled hopes for the shot that would never come down. And indeed the cry came down from space, ". . . it's sailing for miles and miles and miles," Alan Shepard was giving the mad cry of golfers the world over who want to put a ball in orbit and reassume their god-like power.

Yes, indeed, indeed, Shivas was right; the game keeps giving us glimpses.

The Inner Body

A. As Experience

When Shivas gave me that midnight lesson and whispered his instructions to "ken yer inner body" I sensed his meaning at once, even though my "good mind" kept raising questions. Most psychologists would say that he was merely reinforcing my kinesthetic or proprioceptive sense, making me more aware of the messages coming from my muscles and enteroceptors. Or they might say he was making me more sensitive to "the body image," the fluctuating gestalt that emerges from our various bodily sensations. They would thereby reduce it all to proportions which their psychology could manage, for psychologists are generally conscientious people quite concerned to keep man's psyche orderly and comprehensible, and God knows, they have a hard time with the limited tools and maps they have. Concepts like the "inner body" or the "higher self" give most of them enormous difficulty: the Irons-MacDuff Psycho-Cosmology as a whole would give them a very bad time indeed.

But that night Shivas was turning my attention to much more than the kinesthetic sense or the "body image," though these are related to it. For him, the inner body was more than metaphor or "experiential construct." It was a vivid undeniable reality forever impinging on our workaday world. And once you paid attention to it, it was a doorway to marvelous realms.

Psychologies other than our twentieth-century Western model include these dimensions of human experience, and have included them for thousands of years. It has been helpful for me to remember that. Indian psychology, for example, has much to say about the *sukshma sharira*, the so-called "subtle" or "feeling" body; the Upanishads describe various *koshas* or "soul-sheaths"; Hindu-Buddhist contemplative practice has given birth to elaborate systems of inner anatomy, full of *nadis* and *chakras* and *Kundalini* powers. These esoteric anatomies correspond in significant ways to similar systems in the lore of Africa, China, and the American Indian nations. Not only has there been a perennial philosophy, there has also been a *perennial anatomy* of the inner body. Lately, these ancient discoveries have been finding their way into the outskirts of our cautious Western psychology. They were bound to find their way there eventually, given the fundamental and irrepressible power of the realms they point to.

Now let us look more carefully at the term we are dealing with. The first word points to the subjective nature of the phenomena and also to the fact that this other body, this *inner* body, is somehow enclosed or placed within our ordinary physical frame. But here the term can be misleading. For as Shivas described it and as I have experienced it, the inner body is not bound to the physical frame it inhabits. It is far more elastic and free, more like a flame than a rock. The term *body* can also be misleading, since body connotes boundary. In Shivas Irons' sense of the term your inner body has no final boundary, unless it is that final paradoxical line in the "bounded infinite." It is a center to operate from, an indubitable *something*, to be sure, but it wavers and dances like a living flame and stretches at times to alarming proportions. It may hurtle through star-gates and openings in time. It/we may suddenly come out in another place, in another body. It/we may merge into everything at once.

Defining the term is a frustrating job. The intellect is often frustrated when it encounters phenomena like these. You need poetry, mathematics, philosophy, and music to approach them. Then your own fantasy can take on the task, drawing you into the reality itself.

We were coming down one of the final fairways toward Burningbush Town. In the silence and the softening light I felt a quiet exaltation. The golf course was still as a quiet lake and as I walked along I heard a sound—a popping of the inner ear, or a cricket—I could not tell where it came from. As I walked along the sound continued, it was impossible to tell if it was coming from within my head or from a distance. Gentle and rhythmic, it sent tiny waves of pleasure through me.

The experience was a first lesson in boundaries, for when I got to the green Shivas asked if I could hear the evening bells from the cathedral. As he asked the question I heard that sound change place, from somewhere inside me to the old church tower. Explaining its origin had created a boundary between it and me.

A similar thing happened during our midnight lesson. As I fell into the focus Shivas wanted, my body widened until it embraced the ball all the way to the target. He had said that the club and the ball are one. "Aye ane fiedle afore ye e'er swung," I can still remember the way he said it, and sure enough I became that field. The first time it happened, I felt the ball hit my stomach as it hit the wall of the ravine, a solid blow that felt like a child's fist. I told him what had happened and he said that he had felt it too.

Like true gravity, the inner body stands outside our ordinary Western view of things. It is real in a way conventional Western psychology will never admit—until psychologists enter these realms themselves.

Artists and poets have seen it more clearly. El Greco's saints or his "View of Toledo" shudder upwards into the living vortex of the sky. "The gallop of his rhythms runs away with the sense," an eminent art critic says; the energy of the inner body is breaking through, drawing everything with it, including the critic's mind. The German painter Matthias Grünewald was more conscious and deliberate about it. Many of his figures are enveloped in aureoles and glories, you can see their subtle bodies made explicit. When he was alive, in those late medieval years, auras, halos and the occult were accessible to the common culture; the artist had seen them or knew a local witch or saint who did. Either he or someone he knew conversed with angels and demons. But as religion waned and worldly skepticism flourished, this subtle vision turned to artifice and mere convention—halos flattened into golden beanies, angels turned to dumplings. What did you do with your saint's nimbus when he turned sideways, show it in two dimensions or three? No one knew *what* they looked like now.

Our contemporary artist invents his own ways of mirroring the inner man. Picasso's "Guernica" is such a device for rendering the psychic mutilation, agony, and terror of war in the twentieth century. The inner body can be torn and rent, pieces of it can be splattered against the wall. Mental hospitals are full of such carnage, so are broken homes and ghetto streets. Have you ever felt it, a piece of your substance blasted away? Why do we say our heart is *broken* or our personality is *split*? These old clichés point to the mutilation of our very substance, to gaping wounds in the inner body that impress themselves irresistibly on our physical guts. We have all felt it. Picasso holds up a mirror to our battle-twisted souls.

Artists and poets who reveal these things may say they are only making metaphors or symbols, but the pictures they make have power because they suck us toward real shapes and forces, because they bring invisible worlds into this one. I think that is the reason some people grow weary at museums and art shows. Boredom can be a defense against dark intrusions. For:

> The Ghosts, and Monster Spirits, that did presume
> A Bodies Priv'lege to assume,

> Vanish again invisibly,
> And Bodies gain agen their visibility.

The metaphysical poet was describing the light of day-break—and suggesting dark transferals and passageways from this world to another.

B. As Fact

In the Stanford University library there is an enormous collection of books on mysticism and the occult. The founder's brother, Thomas Walton Stanford, developed an interest in these matters and donated large sums of money to the university for their study. He also sent long shelves of theosophical writings, and a case of apports to his brother's school. (An apport is a materialization of the ectoplasm or subtle substance emanating from a séance with the dead.) Through the years I have explored this towering collection, spending many a day leafing through dusty books hardly opened since they were printed, and have discovered that research into the phenomena of the inner body has been going on incessantly since the founding of the British Psychical Research Society in 1882. I would estimate that several thousand independent inquiries have been conducted to see what reality there is in the ancient reports about auras, telepathy, clairvoyance, survival of bodily death, and related matters. The American and British Psychical Research societies have accumulated, in their journals, annals, and proceedings, reports that are staggering in number and impressive in method. If these people can be trusted—and many of them like William James have been respected in other fields of inquiry—the evidence is compelling that we do indeed possess another body, an *inner* body, a vehicle of consciousness that survives death, travels to far places during sleep and trance, and changes size and shape. It can be seen by certain clairvoyants and be made to appear to unsuspecting persons like an apparition. There is a perennial anatomy of this subtle body, and many attempts have been made to organize the knowledge about its structure and functioning. One such attempt, a kind of *Gray's Anatomy* of the soul entitled *Human Personality and Its Survival of Bodily Death*, was compiled by Frederic Myers, the neglected genius of psychical research who invented the word "telepathy" and other terms used by parapsychologists. And there are other compilations of past research and belief about the occult too numerous to list, but you can explore for yourself by reading any book on ESP with a bibliography and fanning out from there. One book leads to another, and if you go on, you will find yourself wandering in a world of inquiry, speculation, and adventure more vast than you ever would have imagined. You will see the teeming underside of our Western rationalism and science.

C. As Luminous Body

Shivas and his teacher had elaborated a theory that for nearly every major invention in recent times there was a corresponding power man could develop in his own being without needing a mechanical or other external contrivance. For example, we could learn to fly without airplanes once we fell into "true gravity" and learned to breathe properly (or hit fantastic golf shots with Irish shillelaghs when we mastered the secrets of the "inner body"). This, of course, is an ancient idea, going back to alchemy, Gnosticism, and the Vedic Hymns of India.

"Oh Son of Energy," says the *Rig-Veda* (VIII, 84.4), referring to the primal Consciousness-Force that underlies all things and dwells in the human soul, "other flames are only branches of thy stock." At the heart of human consciousness is the same power that "is in the waters and the forests, in things stable and in things that move, even in the stone. . . ." The Vedic rishis believed that through this basic connection in our soul with Agni (the Primal Fire), man could evoke and assume Its power. As you discovered this profound connection, they said, you would begin to grow into the Being from which everything sprang. And as you did, certain manifestations of that Being would begin to appear in your life. Your body, for example, would begin to glow with the First Light. This assumption of inward powers has been glimpsed by El Greco in his pictures of the saints, in Byzantine mosaics shimmering with golden aureoles. The emanation of light from within, in fact, became a convention for many centuries of Western art, codified in *mandorlas*, nimbuses, and glories, in halos of varying sizes and shapes.

Energy was another sign of the transformation, how else to account for the fact that Shivas Irons and Seamus MacDuff seemed rarely to sleep, starting legends about themselves throughout the Kingdom of Fife? Energy, as relativity theory and other formulations of modern physics say, has something to do with structure: this is how I account for the weird perception I had when Shivas hit his shot that day on the thirteenth tee. Something extraordinary happened there, even though a shutter in my brain snapped shut before I could comprehend it. My impression is that it had to do with the structure of the entire hole and its relation to Shivas's body. Whatever it was that he triggered, there can be no doubt that some incredible energy had manifested itself, without the intervention of atom smashers or other machinery.

The transcendence of ordinary gravity is a privilege of the luminous body, say the journal notes. "If I ever breathe with it, I will fly across the ravine," is an enigmatic saying I found the other day. (I am not sure what the "it" refers to.) There are other references to flying in the notes. Shivas was trying to identify with the ball in flight for several months, to incorporate its trajectory into his inner being; he meditated on sea gulls as they skimmed the waves off Burningbush; he played with all sorts of mathematical formulas concerning gravity and its relation to music. Most of all, he was working to bring the inspiration of the inner freedom directly into his body. He called his trances "the trip up" and his work on the body "the trip down," because his cells were slowly being altered by the primal force he brought from his ecstatic states. (There was a similar emphasis in Aurobindo's work, hence his appreciation of the Indian seer.)

In one passage he speculates about his bodily organs being transmuted into luminous centers that would do the job our ordinary parts were secretly aspiring to do. ". . . heart into warming fire, lungs into wings, sexual organs into flaming swords of love. . . ." The body itself was being turned to gold in his joyous alchemy.

Some Notes on True Gravity

When I began work on this book I was tempted to make a glossary of terms from the Irons-MacDuff cosmology, but soon realized that what they were talking about was too complex for straight-line definitions. What you really need to explain "true gravity," for example, are photographs (such as the ones Shivas had in his room), mathematical demonstrations, music, and inspired chapters of poetic philosophy. But this would still be inadequate: a round of golf with Shivas Irons would finally be needed to comprehend it in depth, or a night in Seamus's ravine with the "baffing spoon."

There are other terms in Shivas's private vocabulary which are roughly synonymous with "true gravity." For example: "feeling-force," "heart power," and the Sanskrit philosophical word *chit*, which is sometimes translated as "consciousness-force." Other related terms and phrases appear less frequently in my notes and memory, e.g., Gravity-with-Loving-Eyes, shimmering Body-Field, a MacDuff-Body, a Pythagorean Unit, a PK Field (or Psychokinetic Field), breathing baffing spoon, Galactic-Ecstatic-Hole-in-One, eighteen holes on the "milky fairway" (Shivas saw golfing figures in the starry heavens), and, of course, all the words having to do with the "inner body."

As you can see from these various phrases, true gravity connotes the joining of awareness, delight, and embracing-force. According to Shivas, these are joined at most levels of existence, but our modern world and its dominant philosophies work to separate them. True gravity is, on the one hand, an experiential reality; it is also a force-at-large in the world, the omnipresent "heart power" or "feeling-force" that permeates all things. It is the dynamic aspect of the one Omnipresent Reality, like the *shakti* of the Tantric school of Hindu and Buddhist philosophy. It is this double nature of the idea that makes it so strange to our Western sensibility, for we have learned to internalize the ordinary scientific notion of force as something separate from consciousness and feeling. We may speak of "personal force," "weight of character," and "the gravity of a situation," but these are generally regarded as mere metaphors.

Gravity as described by Sir Isaac Newton is a concept rendered with mathematical equations which are used to achieve certain feats of prediction and control in the physical sphere. "True gravity" connotes force, but it is also a highly aware entering and joining of those "swarming fields" that make up our universe. It would bring our overcontrolling manipulative ways back into harmony with nature on all its levels, animate and inanimate. It is good for man to assume power, but power joined to consciousness (as Pythagoras had intended), power "in the Will of God."

Which leads to another term in the Irons-MacDuff cosmology, namely, "the next manifesting plane." The world is always tending toward some new and fuller being, and true gravity is a way into it. GOD IS WAKING UP was the title of one of his charts. The mentality of ordinary Western science is ultimately a dead end because it is only in touch with part of that emerging reality; it is only a thin slice of God's Will. "How-to" golf books were part of the tendency of the modern mind to rely solely on technique, hence Shivas's primary reliance on true gravity and the inner body in his golf instruction.

True gravity is a universal force, an ethical imperative, and an overwhelming spiritual experience.

True gravity is intentional. That is, once you enter these realms you cannot will any result arbitrarily; you must learn to join your will to the emerging will of God, or to put it another way, you must place yourself in ecological harmony with the awakening world, not the "old-static-dying-world" but to the "next manifesting plane" as it develops in and around you. Modern science is a kind of black magic that tries to lord it over nature from a limited and inadequate consciousness: like all black magic it produces an "occult backlash" that will bring the world down unless it is tempered and eventually subsumed by the kind of consciousness Shivas was aspiring for. God intends the fullness of His being in the world, not just a thin slice, so "He will bring down the modern mind like a fallen species and clear the way for His greater life." That line sent shivers up my back when I read it. Today it seems more prophetic still.

There are endless symptoms of body, mind, and spirit, he said, when we fail to align ourselves with this beckoning power, "a thousand painful warnings that we are off the path." Once we sense its true intention, ". . . there are always signals enough to steer by." He was working on a "Hamartiology of Golf," a science of our misalignment, to help his students learn the way.

It is an adventure of unimaginable consequence and splendor, this discovery of true gravity, and "we quaver in its presence." Modern technology and hedonism, say my Scottish wizard-teachers, are defenses against its ecstasy and light. They are "hazards where the match might end."

Shivas's journals were full of hints about that adventure: one section described "the streamers of energy that guide any golf shot hit in true gravity." The path I visualized spontaneously for my first shots at Burningbush were anticipations, I now think, of a more deliberate process of visualization he was teaching MacIver; I was picking up on his lessons unconsciously. Many golfers do this, perhaps you do; Shivas was developing it into consummate art. Visualization of the ball's path could lead to actual streamers of energy emanating from the golfer to the target, streamers upon which the golf ball traveled. One reason for the quiet surrounding the game is that players and onlookers alike sense that something occult is under way and that they should not interfere. For, as the notes go on, ". . . they [the energy streamers] can be affected by the player or the gallery."

The notes continue, ". . . suddenly I have new powers and apprehensions, invisible arms like Shiva, everyone senses it. Campbell and MacIver half-sensed that I was swinging with extra legs and arms today, inner body wide as a green. Indian artists showed us . . . not until lately our Western artists who, like science, fit into the Western world. . . . imagine God, how does he hold the world since He *is* the world in all its parts? All our scientists could imagine how God *holds* us, practice it in school, in their laboratories, at least ask for guidance. My golf students can do it, some of them. How did God get this earth-ball rolling? True gravity permeates the universe, He holds it all in Shiva's arms."

". . . Newton divided his work into scientific and occult-religious studies, went along with the European split . . . his good crazy side fell asleep. He and his scientific world held their other voices down, amen, establishing themselves as competent men. Their forgotten murmurings: in finding the way for Western science they were ever in touch with the darker fullness but tailored what they sensed to the culture of their time. Science growing up. Competent men. Seamus says he will study Newton's forgotten papers about the history of the world."

"A True Idea has arms to embrace. True Ideas are a body's and a culture's invisible center. Mathematics are invisible . . . [my writing was indecipherable here] . . . streamers of light."

Occult Backlash

The wisdom of my Scottish teacher suggests that there are lines of intention guiding all our human experience. These ever so gentle "psychokinetic" fields become more apparent as we grow sensitive to life's messages and vibrations. There is sometimes a temptation to manipulate them before we know their full intent, but we can only follow their lead and yield to their unfoldment. When we do not, when we try to turn them to our small advantage (which is our large disadvantage), they come back to claim us for their larger purpose. Their occult principles are yet to be understood, the results of tampering with them are still unpredictable. When they are not approached with love and modesty they lash back.

When I willed my shots with all my might on the early holes at Burningbush I damaged my clubs, my ball, my score, my good humor, my relationship with MacIver and Shivas. A part of me—my scheming imagination—was going faster than my other parts, "faster than the Lord," in the words of an older psychology. In his notes Shivas refers to psychic "carom shots" and "occult backlash." These result when power is applied from inadequate love and awareness. They operate in all dimensions of life.

Something happened to me ten or twelve years ago that brought me back to his thoughts on the subject with a jolt. It happened in the most innocent of circumstances, at a base-ball game.

The San Francisco Giants were playing the Los Angeles Dodgers on a cold and windy night, a typical night at Candlestick Park. I had gone to the game with three friends, in high spirits, determined to root our team to victory and prevail over the bitter weather. Jack Sanford, the Giants' best pitcher then, was going against the nearly unbeatable Sandy Koufax. In those days I had developed a set of whammies to use against opposing teams, a whole array of cries and gestures reminiscent of cartoons about voodoo witch doctors. As cheer-leading devices they often worked to perfection: George Leonard and I had once timed a war cry so well that Bob Gibson fell on his posterior while delivering a pitch, something he had never done before according to the next day's *Sporting Green*. (There was no doubt about his fall being provoked by our well-timed cry.) On occasion I would get the people sitting near us to use these gestures too. Usually they wouldn't, out of either embarrassment or common decency. Once, in fact, a man had been so offended by my performance that he had hit me a karate chop on the back of the head. But on this particular night everyone around joined in. I told some of them that the gestures had been developed by shamans in the Amazon basin to kill their enemies, one in particular in which the two middle fingers were doubled back under the thumb with index finger and little finger extended like evil horns toward the target. Various movements of the hands could sharpen the emanation. It was my most successful night as a cheerleader. By the third inning there were perhaps two hundred rooters practicing this form of Amazon witchcraft on Sandy Koufax and the unsuspecting Dodgers. At two points in the game I grew dizzy from the excitement we were causing.

It soon became obvious that our devil's rooting section was having its effect. The Dodgers began to make weirdly inept plays whenever we got a strong wave of gestures and curses going. Several hundred sets of evil horns pointed toward the diamond. But Koufax, being the phenomenal pitcher he was, was hard to budge. Inning after inning went by and there was still no Giants' run. Toward the middle of the game the Dodgers scored once, in spite of our psychic fire-storm. We were going like fury though, working ourselves into shamanistic possession, all two hundred of us out in section 17. I thought I might faint, the energy was running so high.

Then came the first omen. Jack Sanford was forced to retire from the game in the seventh inning, even though he had held the Dodgers to one run, because "something had happened to his arm." Jack Sanford was ineffective for the rest of the season. In fact, he was never any good again.

But our furious gestures and shouts continued. We had by now helped stimulate the entire crowd to frenzy. Into the ninth inning we went, still behind 1 to 0, riding the excitement we had started like the troops of Genghis Khan. We were getting better and better at timing our shots. Then with a crescendo of awful howls and laughter, we finally broke the Dodgers' hold: in the last of the ninth the Giants scored twice and victory was ours. I staggered out of the stadium suspecting that I had almost given myself a heart attack, a psychically depleted witch doctor.

The next morning I opened the *Chronicle Sporting Green* to read about the game. The first thing I saw was a very small article, a little filler, at the bottom of the page. It said "Michael Murphy dies at Giants' game." The article briefly told how one Michael Murphy, aged seventy-two, had died of a heart attack that night at Candlestick Park.

"Psychic carom shots," "occult backlash"; naturally I remembered Shivas's words. Had I murdered poor old Mike Murphy? You might think about it if something similar happens to you.

A Golfer's Zodiac

One starry night during the war Shivas rediscovered the zodiac. The "true zodiac" he called it, since it bore little resemblance to the one your ordinary astrologer refers to. He did not see it *all* that night, in fact there was still a constellation missing when I met him fifteen years later. But during his lonely nighttime vigils he looked up there and eventually put most of it in place.

It had thirteen signs. An extra one was needed, he said, to fit the stars to our new age. As in other spheres science was badly out of touch here. We were passing now from the age of Shank to the age of MacDuff; he had named the governing constellation of the coming age after his teacher. Reading round the heavenly circle, the signs went like this: Burningbush (where Aries had been), the first sign of spring, then Porky Oliver, Morris and Morris (after Tommy, Jr., and Old Tom), Vardon, Jones, Slice, one unnamed, Hook, Disappearing Hole, Swilcan Burn (after a famous golf hazard), Hogan, MacDuff, and Shank. These were the configurations marking his "milky fairway." He had been born, I believe, on the cusp between Hogan and MacDuff, hence his enormous regard for them both.

The most interesting sign as far as I am concerned was "Disappearing Hole." I thought about it after I saw the movie *2001: A Space Odyssey*, for it was something like the stargate through which the astronaut plunged toward his shattering transformation. Apparently it was the sign Shivas peered into first during his nocturnal meditations, at least when it was in the sky. For all I know, he was looking for it that night on the window ledge. He related it to the mystery of the hole in golf, our willingness—our passion even—to humble ourselves to that tiny opening after ranging "far and wide across the green world." Star-gate and golf hole, two symbols of Man's crossing through, I wish I could make it out on a clear night. But I have trouble with all the signs he showed me, even though he took great pains to point them out.

It was good to hear that we were passing out of the terrible age of Shank. The past centuries, like the dreadful golf shot after which they were named, were the very worst in civilization's troubled history; we could look forward now to an age of "true gravity" and the apotheosis of his teacher's vision. Hook and Slice had been other bad eras in the world's unfoldment. The Age of Jones had been a good one.

If my memory is correct, he said I had several planets in Swilcan Burn—though my birthdate fell on the cusp between Slice and the unnamed sign. He could tell just by looking at me that the planets were there, and this meant that I was always in danger of ending in the final hazard. Though he pronounced upon the fact with great solemnity and conviction, I have never been able to remember what the "final hazard" was.

I asked him why he didn't name that last sign, seeing that he could always change it later if it didn't seem right. But he shook his head decisively and said that every sign made itself known "when he was ready." Naming a constellation "was nae little thing."

Hogan and Fleck in the
1955 U.S. Open

Many players have a natural sense of their inner body and true gravity, according to Shivas. Nearly everyone has had a glimpse or two. Certain players must have had an especially great sense of it, he thought, especially Ben Hogan. In 1955 he had made his one and only trip abroad, to see about living and teaching in America when Seamus died, and during the trip he had seen the U. S. Open Championship at the Lakeside course in San Francisco. He had followed Hogan through all four rounds, until the final tie with the then unknown Jack Fleck. He said that Hogan was centered in the "fourth and sixth chakras," psychic centers near the heart and between the eyes. He emanated a presence that could be felt by any sensitive observer, in fact it had affected the entire gallery. He was part-way into true gravity, it seems.

Shivas had followed him up the clubhouse steps after the final round, to "experience his presence at close range." He had followed Hogan into the dressing room, pushing his way through guards and officials as if he belonged there. He said that Hogan seemed to recollect himself as if by long habit, "almost like a monk." Reporters and some of the other players had gathered to congratulate him on the first-ever fifth U. S. Open title. But Hogan would not accept the congratulations. He had reluctantly held up five fingers for Gene Sarazen and the television cameras out on the eighteenth green because Sarazen had coaxed him into doing it. But now he would not get his hopes up, no—not until victory was certain. The even attitude never wavered, even now in the moment of victory, his composure was so deeply rooted. Then, according to Shivas, an enormous cheer went up outside and Hogan swore, his equanimity broken for one angry phrase. He knew that Fleck, an entirely unknown professional, had tied his score, that a playoff would be necessary. But then, Shivas said— seeing hidden meanings everywhere—Hogan automatically snapped back to "the fourth *chakra*."

A little later he found himself sitting on a couch upstairs with Hogan's wife—synchronicity having led him there— when the champion appeared, composed as ever, gracious and smiling to his friends, as centered as he was on the course.

Fleck started telling the press he had discovered Hogan's "secret." But he wouldn't tell what the secret was. Some speculated that it was the "pronation" Hogan had introduced into his swing to prevent hooks, but Fleck wouldn't say. Even Hogan couldn't figure it out the next day during the play-off. Shivas, however, as you might expect, knew what it was. It was Hogan's own presence, communicated directly to Fleck: the champion's "inner body" had emanated directly to the younger professional, so much so that Jack Fleck won that U. S. Open title. Hogan was a true teacher but an unconscious one, said Shivas, the mental part of his game had come so naturally. Just as Sam Snead was a natural "physical golfer," Hogan was a natural "in the psychic sphere."

As far as I know, Hogan was Shivas's chief golf hero. He had a theory that the great champion was not meant to win a fifth U. S. Open title, because he had to pass "the secret" on. An occult process was working itself out teacher to teacher— Shivas and Jack Fleck were now part of the circulation of the golfing light. I have often wondered if some of it was passed along to me.

I think it is good to remember that the mental states these unusual methods induce are familiar to golfers the world over. And I thought it might reassure you to know that Ben Hogan has been involved in these occult matters all along.

A Hamartiology of Golf

How the Swing Reflects the Soul

Peter McNaughton had remarked that nowhere does a man go so naked as he does before a discerning eye all dressed for golf. Shivas recalled the remark and asked me if I knew the word "hamartia." (I can hear his broad Scots accent shading at times into the King's English he had learned in his few years of formal schooling.)

"It originally meant bein' off the taraget, in archery or some such," he said, "and then it came to mean bein' off the taraget in general in all yer life—it got to mean a flaw in the character. Now I dinna' have to tell ye that the body and the mind are *both* parts o' the character, so when a man swings he tells us all about himself. Ye take MacIver now. He's a marvelous methodic man, but damn he tries so hard, I dinna' like to ask him out to dinner. He's not much fun. He'll niver be a brilliant one, but he's got that bulldog will and 'll probably learn somethin' about true gravity before he's through." I thought of our playing partner and his absolute devotion to every maxim laid down by his teacher. Images of other people I knew began to parade before me.

"Ye see, the basis for a change in the way a person plays the game must be laid in his entire life. Now take this talk about keepin' yer eye on the ball. Everyone talks about it, it's almost the first rool o' the game. But there's so much more to it than simply lookin' there a' that little thing, yer whole life is there, man, in the way ye do it, ye bring yer entire past into every shot. It's all written there in yer bones and muscles and

157

nerves. Ye take a man who aye looks down the fairway before he's e'en turned into the ball, why I'll show ye how he does it in everything else in his life." He stood to demonstrate the movement of overanticipating during a golf swing, jerking his head and shoulders up as his hands came into the ball. He pretended to stumble back against his chair.

"Now take every other kind o' error." He began to list them. "Lungin; now how does the fellow lunge into things generally? Maybe he disna' have energy enough to get any power, or maybe he hasna' learned that power comes with waitin'." He brought his hands down gracefully into the imaginary ball, as if waiting for the club head.

"Or blowin' up, he disna' ken what to do with excess energy or frustration or fidgetin'. God, I've seen players who fidget get back in the bar and keep jumpin' around—*nae center at a'!*

"Or boastin', God, what bores some o' them are. An enormous ratio o' talk to skill. Compulsive talkers, recallin' every feeble accomplishment, ye think they were heroes parring that one hole. They're usually in bad health, I've noticed. Haven't learned to get the feelin' into their bodies, it's so bottled up in their words.

"Ye can tell a lot by listenin' to the sounds a man makes, all the grunts and breathin's around a green or on the tee. Sometimes I close my eyes to heer my pupils better—ye might try it yersel' sometime, just listenin' to yer foursome as if 'twere a piece o' music. Are they makin' good music or bad, just try listenin'." He then described the varieties of sound he was talking about, various grunts, squeaks, and cries of the golfing world—I was amazed at the wealth of example he gave and its obvious accuracy. A golf course does give off an exhalation of sound that tells a lot about its clientele.

"Yes, a man's style o' play and his swing certainly reflect the state of his soul," he resumed his description of golfing hamartia. "Ye take the ones who always underclub. The man who wants to think he's stronger than he is. D' ye ken any-body like that?" He raised one quizzical eyebrow. "Think about the rest of his habits. Is he always short o' the hole?"

"Then there are the ones who are always owerclubbin' and landin' on the next tee. It's an X-ray of the soul, this game o' gowf. I knew a married fellow from London who kept a girl goin' here in town, a real captain's paradise. Well, damned if he didn't keep two score cards for a round, one for the first nine and one for the second. And changed his balls for the second nine too, just like he did in real life. I wonder which scorecard he showed to his wife?

"I could give ye hundreds o' examples. Someone could put an encyclopedia together about it. Tak' the lads who run around the course with nae ability to enjoy the game or their surroundin's oor their friends. Some o' them have heart at-tacks on the uphill holes. One man owns a couple of restau-rants in Dundee, big promoter, out o' breath all the time. I won't play with him any mair. And he certainly has nae time for me. I've learned these hurryin' types can hardly wait to take their putts, especially the short ones. That's the time to make 'em a bet—ye can win a pile knowin' that." He paused, shaking his head. "There is a right speed for playin' the game, a right speed. And for living all the rest o' the day.

"Then there's the man who can't stand prosperity. One or two good holes and he's beginnin' to imagine the worst. Ah take 'im home and get 'im to act out his catastrophic expecta-tions and practice some meditation.

"If I were to paint a picture o' the gowfin' world, it'd look like the Hell o' Hieronymus Bosch. Ye ken that's what he was really paintin'."

"Bosch!" I exclaimed.

"Bosch," he said, gravely nodding his head. "Toorns out he was a gowfer too, played a game called *kolven*. Ye can see it when ye look at the picture o' Hell in his 'Garden of Earthly Delights.'"

There was not a trace of doubt in his voice that Bosch had

played the game and drawn inspiration from it. I have a copy of the famous triptych and look at it from time to time to comprehend his words more fully. The panel on Hell does seem to reflect the agonies I have seen on many a golf course.

The Rules of the Game

The thought of Shivas Irons playing golf sometimes strikes me as an utter absurdity. Can you imagine other philosophers and mystics out on the course? Saint Francis, for example, laboring over a 3-foot putt, or Plato slinging a bag of clubs over his shoulder and striding happily down the first fairway. How a spirit so mad for the deeper mysteries could devote a life to this frustrating sport is a question that still distracts me. I sometimes grow vague at dinner parties when I think about it. And when I think of his passion for keeping score and following the rules I am sometimes led to ponder the final absurdity. The thought of him counting all eleven strokes I took during that hole at Burningbush still bogles my mind. "Michael, I think 'twas eliven." I will never forget those words and the image of faithful MacIver writing it down as if the number would be engraved on some Rosetta stone.

How a spirit so large would confine itself to things so small is the kind of paradox that gives birth to philosophy. Life in its tormenting wisdom must have given it to me for a reason, I tell myself, perhaps as a koan, delivered by some guardian spirit at the proper moment. It is significant perhaps that I met him on my way to India in search of the Infinite Mind.

Thinking about this paradox, I realize how fascinated he was with the mystery of the hole in golf. "Do ye know any other game where ye roam so far and wide to reach such a tiny goal?" he asked us all that night. "Why do we submit to such a thing?" He was speaking for himself, not us, for no one else at the McNaughtons' that night had so given themselves to the game. But the question is still with me. Why we choose such an anally frustrating outcome for such a wide-ranging game is a puzzler; Hogan for one has sometimes said that putting should be abandoned, that it ruins an otherwise exciting game. Does it reflect some profound constipation in the Scottish and Anglo-Saxon character? One has to wonder. But more basic to golf's paradoxical nature than putting and the spectacle of that tiny hole at the end of all our endeavors is the utter devotion to rules and exact scorekeeping that all true golf lovers maintain. "To cheat is to end the game," say the journal notes.

What is the reason for this scrupulous honesty, I ask myself, having doctored my own scores for years in endlessly ingenious ways. Does it spring from the bottomless need to test and prove oneself which is so apparent in all man's quixotic endeavors on mountain tops and outer space—or in ravines with baffing spoons? That certainly has something to do with it. Is it a way to prove yourself good to the parent within, to the court of law society has planted in your brain, is it a way to alleviate the guilt we feel just being alive? Yes, we nod in agreement, that could well be part of the reason for such scrupulous trials. But these motives, certain as they may be, are not enough to explain my teacher's horror at golfing dishonesty and his total acceptance of the game's confining structure.

Pondering the question, I have come to think that a person grows in his regard for the rules as he improves his game. The best players come to love golf so much they hate to see it violated in any way. In that they are like anyone who is consummately skilled, be it in the arts, science, or loving their wives. A scientist loves the procedures that give birth to discovery, an artist loves the skills that go into his art, the good man loves the moral dimensions in every act. So Shivas loved the rules and skills of golf. It was a mark of his commitment.

And yet all these explanations, compelling as they may be, do not completely satisfy me. Underlying all the other reasons for his devotion to the game's restraints, I think, is the fact that golf is simultaneously a doorway and a prison, the very mirror of life in that regard. It provides us a jail to be broken out of, but a jail we can clearly see rather than the often invisible one that holds us in our daily life. Shivas always seemed subdued to me when he was indoors, but it was then that his spirit soared in conversation or ecstatic trance to spaces far beyond those enclosed by the room he was in. So it was, I think, with his surrender to the game; its constraints dramatized the situation in which he found himself in this bounded world, it was a place from which to effect a marvelous transcendence.

But there is more to it than that, more than escape is involved. I think of his words about "the trip down," that movement of his soul from the mystic heights "bringing fairy dust into the world." On the practice tee and on the links he was opening himself to subtle energy transferals between the inner and the outer worlds, entering by slow steps into the "luminous body." This amazing alchemy, practiced so faithfully for so many years, was leading to a transformation of his very substance, he said, not a mere escape from this painful earth. Golf was a place for the transformation to unfold.

You might know that the beginnings of this mighty work would occur in such unlikely circumstances, this being such an unlikely world.

On Keeping Score

"Keeping score is a koan, a reminder of the dualities."

"Our relation to paradox is a barometer of our enlightenment."

These two sayings from Shivas's journal give the essence of his attitude toward keeping score. He was scrupulous about counting every stroke, but he was just as insistent that his pupils let the awareness of it recede to the "back of their minds." He sometimes instituted a "second scoring system" for pupils who were having a difficult time with this. He would give them points for certain attitudes and behaviors, to reinforce the changes he wanted. This reconstruction of the scoring system was always done with the player's consent, he said, "to preserve his dignity." For example, MacIver was getting points that day for his unflappability; it "was the strength he had to build on." You will remember how inexorable that golfing tortoise was as he showed me the way to a fine equanimity; well, he was being rewarded for that by Shivas's unforgettable smile. Experts in behavior modification and operant conditioning would have been proud of my obscure Scottish professional's grasp of their science.

You might try making your own "second scoring system," giving yourself points for a calm and centered attitude or for sweetness in the rough. Perhaps a smile after a double bogey or a gracious remark to your playing partner when he beats you would be worth a point. If you know an expert in "behavior mod," as it is called in the trade, you might bring him in.

It is important to remember that your handicap is not an exact mirror of your soul. It is your relation to your score that really counts. A gracious acceptance of your place on the golfing ladder might even help the world in unexpected ways. Many of Shivas's pupils were British men of affairs, he said, secretly swallowing their pride as the Empire dwindled, and since the reconciliation of infinite hopes and limited means was at the heart of all his instruction, he conjectured that he had helped Britain through its painful transition to a humbler, more humane role in the world.

The Pleasures of Practice

Sonny Liston in reminiscing about Shivas said that our departed friend often drew a small crowd of caddies and club members around him when he practiced. "There was somethin' hypnotic about the way he hit those shots," he said. "Worked himself into some kind o' trance out there. Sometimes he would hit balls all day, tradin' stories wi' the boys and givin' 'em tips from time to time. A special provision was made for 'im to use the extra fairway, the members liked his practicin' so much." Seven years after Shivas left Burningbush, Liston was still thinking about how he looked on that practice tee, about the look on his face.

I can imagine what an experience it must have been to watch the subtle transformations that were taking place. That magnificent swing being refined even further, a piece of earth being slowly enveloped in the subtle stuff of the inner worlds. Though most of his onlookers had no clear idea about what he was doing, they must have sensed the majesty and artistry involved. It would have been a meditation just to have been near him. Liston said that one of the special pleasures in watching him came when he put on a demonstration of "ball steering" in which he would hit deliberate fades, draws, and other special shots. I wonder how many in his audience realized what experiments were being conducted then!

He loved to practice as much as he loved to play. That night in the ravine he told me there was little difference any more between the two activities, "the pleasures of practice had become so profound."

If I had stayed in Burningbush I might have learned more about "the second art" of golf, as one professional I know has called it. But I have salvaged some wisdom on the subject from Shivas's notes and some discoveries of my own. These I present below, with the hope that I will fulfill at least some of the Boswellian task destiny has given me.

We play the game at many levels. Every golfer knows this, once he begins to examine himself from the point of view of the inner body. To some extent we all go in and out of those extraordinary states I experienced that day in 1956. But how deeply we do depends upon us. We must deliberately culti-vate the attitudes and faculties that support such experience; we must practice these things as Shivas did. We need not limit our practice to a golf course, however; we can develop the "inner eye," for example, "at home on a rainy day."

Golf is first a game of seeing and feeling. It can teach you stillness of mind and a sensitivity to the textures of wind and green. The best instructional books have always said this. Golf is also a game to teach you about the messages from within, about the subtle voices of the body-mind. And once you understand them you can more clearly see your "hamartia," the ways in which your approach to the game reflects your entire life. As Peter McNaughton said, "No-where does a man go so naked . . ."

Beyond such openings to the immediate worlds inside and around us lie "true gravity" and those "images that become irresistible paths." I have devoted a section to them below. They are powers that bring the most inspired golf and give us hints of what we may eventually be.

And finally, underlying and interfusing all these is the one presence and delight, the "Higher Self" and its transforming power that "we are looking for through all the others."

Golf is "a game for taking off the seven veils," said Shivas.

"Never think yer first glimpse the last, for there are aye another six." When I told him about my experience on the thirteenth hole he spread his arms as if he were opening a curtain and shook his hands to say the World-to-be-Seen was shuddering with glory. "Ye only saw tha' much," he added, holding his thumb and forefinger an inch apart to suggest how small was the rent in the veil I had seen through.

Keeping Your Inner Eye on the Ball

Imagine a golf ball. Make the image of it as vivid as you can. When anything intrudes upon the image, let it pass. If the golf ball disappears, imagine it again. If it wavers, make it steady. Doing this you can practice keeping your eye on the ball. You can practice in your room on a rainy day.

If you cannot keep something out of your mind, some hive of your soul-skin, when you are practicing this inner sight, get to know the intrusion. What does it show you about yourself and your situation in the world? Exploring the invader can be helpful to your game.

These are two paragraphs from his notes. They describe a technique for developing concentration and stillness in the disorderly mind. As soon as I saw the words I stopped to visualize a golf ball: I could see the word "Titleist" printed on it. Then the image turned to a little spot of dancing light, and I felt myself rising gently upward. I told him what I was experiencing. He said that any image might take on one's latent mood, the feeling that wanted to come to the surface. In my case, it was the effect of all our "galavanting" that caused my inner eye to dance, for my organism wanted to turn toward the restful light of the "higher self." He said to follow its impulse for a moment, then recreate the image of the ball and try again. It was a surprisingly restful and pleasurable experience.

Lately, I have begun to practice the method with regularity and find that it has a definite carry-over onto the course. When I practice seeing the club and ball as one, following his first instruction to me, I sometimes experience the kind of intrusions he described. Letting them pass in meditation has helped me let them pass on the golf course when I am addressing the ball. My awareness of them, of the way they sneak in when I least suspect them, has grown more acute. It is easier now to see the ball and the golf course as one unbroken field, "Aye ane fiedle afore ye e'er swung."

Blending

Aikido is a Japanese art of self-defense. Robert Nadeau is a teacher of this subtle art who lives and works near San Francisco, and in recent months he has helped me bring the principles of it into my golf game. Although he has never played the game himself, he has an amazing grasp of its problems and opportunities. "Blending" for example is a way to join yourself with your opponent's strength in order to divert his attack; when used correctly it turns a fight to a dance. He has shown me how to "blend" my strength with club, ball, and terrain on the course, in the same way I join with attackers during an Aikido class. It works surprisingly well. Perhaps the most impressive thing about it has been the way in which it has helped me adapt my swing to every situation. My repertoire of shots has grown because I have learned to go with the dynamics of air, wind, and slope, using the energies of the situation to help rather than hinder me. Shivas had said to find my "original swing" in every situation, claiming that he never swung the same way twice. It was hard for me to see the deviations in his flawless strokes, but he claimed they were there. The "blending" principle has brought that subtle adaptation of method to situation into play for me.

An old letter Shivas had never mailed to some student or friend was among the papers I photographed in his apartment. It is a small essay on blending.

"Can you see the brook that golfers fear and not fearing

— and will be in harmony
with you as the dog to the
flocker, as the crop to the
farmer. Walking the course you can
learn many things from your
new found friends, the tree
rooted deeply to the ground, firm,
the upper branches swaying as
natural as the breeze flowing
through it. So reflect on your
stance as you pass the tree.
Can you do this, can you see
the brook that golfers fear and
not fearing but feeling can
you put that flowing water
into your swing. The green
grass restful to body, soothing
to soul. Oh it so many paces
that you put on it or is it
a period of rest and calmness
between you and the lay of
your ball. Be the tree rooted,
be the brook flowing, be
the calmness of the green,

but feeling can you put that flowing water into your swing," what a beautiful way to say it. I think of his swing as I read these words and realize what grace and what strength there is in such blending.

There may also be certain unexpected results from a discipline like this. Shivas for example had learned the art of dowsing while meditating on his union with nature. Burningbush Links had begun to dry out after the war and for the first time in its history had required a watering system. During all the centuries of play upon it, rain and mist had preserved its subtle textures, but now with the postwar golfing boom players from every continent were wearing its resilient fairways down. There was violent disagreement in the club over the measures required to keep the course green. Then, at the very height of the crisis, Shivas discovered water at several places on the links themselves. The knowledge had come to him, he said, "through the handle of his five iron": he felt his golfing stick twitch whenever he approached a potential well. He prevailed upon one of his rich admirers to finance a drilling at one of the sites he had found, and, sure enough, water was there. The discovery settled the club dispute, for now there was plenty of water for little expense. The members had given him a plaque for his help. He told me that the first twitch of his five iron came when he was practicing the kind of blending I have just described.

Becoming One Sense Organ

There is a psychological phenomenon in which one sense modality is stimulated when an impression is received by another, as for example, when the feel of a well-hit golf shot starts a melody in your inner ear. Poets have written about seeing bird songs or hearing flowers blossom. Last season at the San Francisco Forty-Niners-Atlanta Falcon football game I heard Wagner's "Ride of the Valkyries" as the Forty-Niners rallied to win in the fourth quarter. Religious literature is full of similar reports, like the Italian saint's description of colored lights when he heard songs of worship in the village church. For Shivas Irons this mingling of the senses was one of the pleasures of practice.

In his journals he recommends that you try to cross your senses deliberately, as when he says to see *and* feel "the club and ball as one unbroken field" or to "hear the breaking waves when you hit a bag of practice balls."

Bobby Jones often heard a melody through a round of golf and followed its rhythm when he swung; Shivas recommends something like that when he says to "hear the inner sounds and rhythms and let them enter your play." Sometimes such synesthesias carry an informative message, sometimes they are simply there to be enjoyed. I will never forget that experience on the thirteenth hole at Burningbush, when all my senses joined. For a moment then I was one sense organ: the world was a single field of music, joy, and light.

Some of Shivas's exercises remind me of the centering techniques in Paul Reps's little book *Zen Flesh, Zen Bones.* These are taken from Tantric disciplines which used the natural impulses as pathways to enlightenment: behind each impulse there is a higher possibility, the Tantric philosophers said. For example, the journal notes suggest that "when the fear of failure steals over you imagine the bottom of your mind dropping out as you fall into the Void." The fear of failure may be a premonition of the liberated state.

Or, "sometimes a path appears in your mind's eye for the ball to follow: let it blend with your body." That, of course, is what happened to me on the very first hole I played with him. But my greed for par blotted the image out.

The Value of Negative Thoughts

One night I was ruminating about my adventure in Burningbush, counting the shots I took during our round of golf (only 34 of them on the back nine), recalling the remarks that were made around the McNaughtons' dinner table, visualizing Shivas's room with its butcher-paper charts and arcane books. As the impressions of that crowded day mingled in my memory a clear gestalt began to emerge, taking for its central image the chart on his wall entitled, GOD IS WAKING UP. Remembering it and the photographs and his memorable sayings, one central theme emerged: that everything in life is potentially something more, that every person, every object, every event is waiting for transformation. Or to put it like he sometimes did, "from your deeper mind everything has an aspiring face."

Now, for most of us, this is a difficult truth. Perhaps because we are not in touch with our "deeper mind," most of what we are confronted with on a given day has no special meaning at all. At best it looks like a battlefield between God and the Devil, with the Devil winning at least half of the time; more often it seems like one damned thing after another. The profoundly optimistic vision underlying the phrase "God Is Waking Up" seems to have little basis in fact, at least the facts as we perceive them. Ah, but there is the catch! If we are honest, we have to say "the facts as we perceive them," thus leaving open the possibility that they may be seen *another* way.

For him everything was full of messages. Nowhere was this so apparent, he said, as it was in golf. And nothing is more informative during a round of golf than the so-called negative thought.

There are two attitudes you can take to these, he maintained; one of detachment and disidentification or one of listening to the perverse voice to see what it may tell you. Many thoughts that arise as you are playing must be brushed aside: there are ways to do that, ways to strengthen "the inner eye." But certain ones that will *not* be brushed aside must be understood, otherwise they will haunt you until your golf game and your disposition suffer. Some years ago a thought like that began to torment me.

It began entering my mind when I was putting. It said, "You are not lined up straight, line up again." It occurred to me over and over that the angle of my putter face was slightly askew. I would stand back and try to line up at a better angle, but still the thought was there. It kept coming back through the entire round. When I played again, a week or so later, the same voice began again— "You are not lined up straight, line up again," it said, creeping into my mind on every green and eventually as I was addressing the longer shots. I adjusted and readjusted my stance, waggled the club endlessly, the greens and fairways began to look like cubistic drawings as I surveyed them for a better line. Then it slowly dawned upon me that the thought was coming from some deep recess of my mind, that it was one of those thoughts Shivas had said I should listen to. What did it have to say? I let it run through my mind after that second round, let it play itself out, "You are not lined up straight, line up again." Slowly, inexorably, the meaning came clear: indeed I was not lined up straight, in my work, with my friends, during most of the day. I was sleeping in my office then, rising to telephone calls concerning the Institute, doing business over every meal. I was as disorganized as I had ever been and my unconscious knew it, and now it was speaking to me clearly on the golf course. I needed to realign my life, it said, not just my putt or my drive. Only during a round of golf did I slow down enough for the word to get through.

As I put my days in better working order, with the help of a "Time Analyst" named Alan Lakein and some invaluable help from my friends, the obsession left me out on the course. Golf had been my therapy.

It is hard to protect yourself from a nagging impulse during a four-hour round of golf—your mind is rarely so exposed. When such a voice begins to speak, it is wise to let it deliver its entire message.

There are also happy obsessions. The other day I could not repress a smile each time I addressed the ball. The higher self was smiling down, telling me to swing just the way I wanted to. I shot a tremendous round and grinned like a kid all the way back to the clubhouse.

"All life is yoga," said the Indian seer Aurobindo. "All golf is yoga" might have been a line from the journals of Shivas Irons. Yoga means joining our deepest self. We may be tending that way, he said, but we need to give the process our deliberate assent to get the ball rolling well. We have to go with all our negative and positive urges, wisely following or guiding them in the Godward direction they want to go.

". . . ugly images are like peyote buttons, they turn into vision." Shivas Irons, *curandero*, with his bag of peyote balls, teaching the unsuspecting people of Burningbush the fundaments of visionary golf!

"The psyche never quits. The messages are always coming. Life is taking us on a mighty journey, if we will only go."

"Driving downwind, follow the shot to infinity." Have you had that sense of it, just for a fleeting second?

Or— "Driving directly into the wind, become the calm solid center." That's a tougher one, but haven't you felt it once or twice? (Among professionals there is an expression "turning the wind around" which refers to the possibility of hitting a long ball into any wind.)

"Walking downhill, become weightless. Walking uphill, slowly become your strength."

There are endless ways to turn an impulse into an exercise. Each of us is given the opportunity every day.

"Imagine the golf ball as a hole in space." The memory of that sentence sprang out at me one day at Lincoln Park, a course on a cliff looking down on the entrance to San Francisco Bay. Fog was rising in slow spires around the red towers of the Golden Gate Bridge and rows of pine and cypress trees lined the fairways like monastery walls.

Through half a round I remembered times when things were giving way: when I was a child locked in a closet shouting for help and the question came "Who am I?" then feeling that I would vanish— "Who am I?" the question was overwhelming me and I repeated my name to hold me there; or fighting a psychic duel with a superior in the Army who was out to get me, thinking I would disappear then; and making love with my head growing dizzy and boundaries falling; these and other images passing through as I walked the fairways between those green sentinel walls and listened to the foghorns in the Golden Gate and watched the ships come into the sunlit sea. Remembering Shivas's words, I saw the ball become a porthole into empty space, with memories of all those fearful glimpses of the Void sorting themselves out for my inner eye. Emptiness within emptiness, protected all around by green grass, good friends, and the blue Pacific hundreds of feet below.

It turned to a crystalline day. And that night another sentence of his pulled the curtains back. "Imagine the stars beneath your feet," I could hear his voice in the ravine as we waited for Seamus.

On Breakthroughs

The greatest breakthrough, Shivas said, was taking your own sweet time to reach the goal, be it par or enlightenment, working all the while with the attitude that any sudden opening comes like Grace, that it is given when the time is ripe and not before. ("The greatest breakthrough is taking forever," was the way he put it.) That does not mean you need practice or aspire any less. On the contrary, it means you can work at your game even more because you will work at it in a way you enjoy.

"*Ohne Hast, ohne Rast,*" he quoted Goethe, "without haste, without rest, be ye fulfilling your God-given hest." I can see him now sauntering down that final fairway with a deep and glowing look, not overly excited by his 320-yard drive to the green, for some new adventure was coming soon.

Against Our Ever Getting Better

But now, before we go any further, let me raise a glass with Shivas as I did that night in Burningbush, and say with all my golfing brothers and sisters, "Fuck our ever getting better."

"Ye'll niver improve yersel', my boy," he roared with glass held high. "How could golf e'er make ye a better person? Just look a' all the ones ye know."

"But that's all you've been talking about," I protested, "our getting better."

"Aw, niver, niver this shitten-gemme," he said with that manly smile. "Just look at Evan thair." He pointed toward the drunken figure across the room, playing an invisible violin. "Do ye ca' tha' self-improvement now! Tae enjoy yersel', tha's the thing," he said, "and beware the quicksands o' perfection." Then he raised his glass of whisky up and shouted, "I say fuck oor e'er gettin' bitter!"

I bring this up because the application of these many exercises in personal growth can lead to a piety and fanaticism he never intended. Crazy for God my teacher may have been, but a gray and lonely one he never was.

As he often said, trying too hard is the surest way to ruin your game.

The Game Is Meant for Walkin'

"Ye're makin' a great mistake if ye think the gemme is meant for the shots," he said with his penetrating look as we sat before Liston's fire in the Burningbush clubhouse. "The gemme is meant for walkin'." He pointed to one of the great Victorian portraits that hung on the wall above us, "And that man there showed us how." The portrait showed an erect, fierce-looking man with a Vandyke beard staring straight ahead like an Indian scout. I imagined him striding down the fairway with that very look, stalking the heathen natives with his shoulders back. He had been a colonel in Queen Victoria's Indian regiments. Shivas could see that I was puzzled.

"Ye see," he continued, "tha' man got to be famous heer for his walkin'. 'Twas said tha' if ye played along wi' him for very long ye'd get the spirit o' it yersel' and learn to enjoy each and every step. 'Twas said tha' he sometimes forgot his shots, the walkin' got to be so good. Had to be reminded by his caddy to hit the ball." He motioned Liston over from the bar and asked him if he had ever known the man in the picture. The jovial barman looked up at the imposing figure and shook his head. He could not remember him; he had come to Burningbush after the old man had died. Shivas went on with his story. "I played with him once when he was ninety yeers old. 'Twas an experience I'll niver firget. He was still walkin' and enjoyin' wi' his clear blue eyes, said he learned to walk like tha' from an Indian yogi back in the 1880s. Went on a walk wi' the yogi into the Himalayas and niver got ower it. Said that a walk like that could be as good for the soul as a day in church, and that was somethin' comin' from him since he was a good Presbyterian. I notice ye hardly pay attention to the walkin' part."

I admitted that I didn't. The next shot usually preoccupied me. Indeed I still have trouble remembering his advice.

"Well, that's too bad," he said as he looked into the fire, "not many people do. 'Tis a shame, 'tis a rotten shame, for if ye can enjoy the walkin', ye can probably enjoy the other times in yer life when ye're *in between*. And that's most o' the time; wouldn't ye say?"

Visualizing the Ball's Flight:
How Images Become Irresistible Paths

When Shivas told me the story of his conversion he said that his obsession with epilepsy and dismemberment was a "prophetic image," a "psychic body" as real as any body we can see. It had emerged from the unconscious, he said, with a power to transform. Such visitations may come to us all at crucial moments of change in our lives. But we do not have to wait passively for their coming; we can deliberately cultivate them to support a discipline, or help us hit a golf shot.

I have already discussed the value of negative thoughts like the one that was telling me to straighten out my life: by letting that voice speak to me clearly, I learned a valuable lesson. Shivas did the same kind of thing when the image of epilepsy exploded in his inner eye and he fell into the ecstatic state that changed his life forever. In both cases the "prophetic image" had to be recognized and accepted before it could do its work.

But images that we *deliberately* foster without any obsessive inward leading can also have a transforming power. Meditation on a golf ball may help you get a sense of life's wholeness, for a sphere is an archetype of perfection (Parmenides thought Being Itself was a globe); or contemplating its diminutive size, the fact that it weighs just an ounce and a half, may lead you to see that in some sense this world is light as a feather, that all life is, as Shivas said, "an earthy nothingness." In his journal he had written that "meditation is an art we need—we lose our way so easily in this teeming world. . . . with eyes open and with eyes closed, on prophetic images and the consequences of our acts, until true gravity takes us up." Along with our inward turnings he would have us stay open to all around us, including the disarray our acts so often bring. On a golf course he was insistent that we follow the flight of every shot to the very end— no matter how bad that shot may be. That is the only way to learn from our mistakes and our successes. It is the only way our unconscious mind can absorb the information it is given; and "we blind ourselves by turning away too soon." (What lessons there for the rest of our life!)

But the most basic kind of meditation during a round of golf is the visualization of our shot as we stand up to the ball.

An image in our mind can become an irresistible path—it happened to me at Burningbush on the very first hole and later in that round after my greed for par had subsided. Many players will tell you they often see their shot before they make it. Many well-known teachers recommend visualization as one of the game's most important secrets.

Shivas said that as you practiced this skill of the inner eye, you would develop a capacity which put forth "streamers of heart power for the ball to fly on." At times it has seemed that my mental picture has changed the direction of a shot after it has left the ground, as if I were steering it from afar.

But these living and tangible images cannot be forced by brute will. Sometimes they form themselves as if guided by a superior intelligence. For example, I saw the path of my ball on the first hole at Burningbush going down the right side of the fairway with a draw, not down the middle as I might have seen it, and so it flew—to the best part of the fairway for an approach to the green. Some invisible radar of my inner body had superseded my ordinary judgment. This has happened to me many times. Through experience you can learn when to stay with your original image and when to yield to the new one.

Whether or not these "streamers" are real remains a question you will have to decide for yourself. They are certainly real in *some* sense. Reality as we ordinarily perceive it is much less rigid than our recent past has taught us.

Shivas Irons' History of the Western World

In the journal notes there was a triple list that went like this:

Inventions	What Could Soon Be	What Will Eventually Be
Airplanes and Automobiles	Ravine Jumps	Full Flight in True Gravity
Telephones	Urgent Telepathic Messages	The Divine Silence
Radio	Sensitive Listening	Universal Clairvoyance and Psychic Mobility
Heating Systems	The Tumo of Tibetan Golfers	The Primal Fire in the Living Soul
Clothes	A Lovely Body	The Power of Emanation and Invisibility
Food Industries	Little Need for Food	Constant Energy Interchange
Newspapers	Intuition of the World's State	Omniscience and Self-Existent Delight
Orchestras	Melodies in the Inner Ear	The Music of the Spheres
Hospitals and Medicine	Bodily Harmony	The Luminous Body
Atom Smashers	Baffing Spoons	Knowledge of the Cracks in Space-Time
Rocket Ships	Astral Flight	Materialization in Another Place
X-Rays	Body Reading	Universal Transparency
Hydrogen Bombs	Psychokinetic Blasts	Explosions of Ecstasy

His handwriting wavered across the page, as if he had been drunk when he wrote it. Maybe he had conceived the list after a rousing night at the McNaughtons'. But whatever the case may be in that regard, it was an example of the kind of thinking he and Seamus were likely to indulge in. For they believed that the direction of Western scientific mastery was only one of several our human race could have taken. In a way, their thinking anticipated that of Herman Kahn and others who like to think about alternative futures. Their main idea about our recent history was that as we accumulate extraordinary inventions to do our work and even some of our play, we gradually lose our latent powers of world-mastery and enjoyment. Behind every invention stands a withered human faculty. One of the reasons Western society took this direction, they maintained, was that the shamans of the West directed themselves to magic and manipulative power, becoming the scientists of our day instead of the luminous sages they had often been in former times. Isaac Newton, for example, obviously suppressed his interest in religion and the occult in his later years; Kepler was a mystic to the end, but focused on those aspects of things the new mania for physical discovery was celebrating; Swedenborg gave full play to his shaman-side but was seen as an oddity. Right down to Robert Oppenheimer the greatest scientific minds put aside their dark intuitions about possibilities of inward knowing—or had them put aside by others. All the inner powers were seen "out there."

When such inquiry began in the West, with Pythagoras and other pre-Socratic Greek philosophers, there was a first sense of the inner-outer joining: Pythagoras had enjoined his followers to grow in soul as they grew in world-knowledge, to "ken the world from within." The Greek sage talked about the music of the spheres, meaning that realm of sound the mystics hear, the *Omkar*, the Original Voice, the birth-song of all the world. Hearing that music you comprehend the octaves and rhythms interfusing all the rest. But to hear it you must surrender, giving yourself over to its pulse of ecstatic love. There is no seeing the world as an object then, for you are joined to the ravishing heart of things, with a memory of God burned in your brain.

But our science only sees the edge of that primary fire, hears only the faint reflection of the primary sound, and so its grasp on the world is mixed and muddling, its outcome still in doubt. "It is a poor lover to this trembling world," said Shivas. "Our hearts cry for deliverance and will not be mocked by half-knowledge, however grand."

"The world is a passage back to God, that is the only reason it is here."

"Hardest matter is consciousness going back, breaking all the bonds as it has for a billion years." The story of our science is a story of mutilated vision, say the Burningbush seers. On one of the charts there was a list of "men who knew," a mind-bogling list running from Pythagoras and Plotinus to Einstein and Henry Ford. It was the crooked golden river of true knowledge running fitfully through our Western centuries. Its title was DANGEROUS CONNECTIONS. The impression you got when you looked at it for a while was that the wires joining our world to God were hopelessly tangled. But at the very bottom there was one hopeful sentence, written in tiny letters: "There is still time," it said.

The Crooked Golden River

A List of People Who Knew

The following list of people is taken from the journal notes. It bore the title I have used above. I do not know what it means exactly, though it seems fairly certain that most of the people listed believed in reincarnation and the evolution of the soul. The list resembles the one on his chart entitled DANGEROUS CONNECTIONS.

"Consider: Lao-tzu, Henry Ford, Mark Twain, Plato, Heraclitus, Pythagoras, Thomas Edison, Thomas Wolfe, Aurobindo, Charles Lindbergh, Goethe, Wordsworth, Coleridge, Salvador Dali, Henry Miller, John Woolman, James Joyce, Yeats, AE, George Bernard Shaw, Oscar Wilde, Gen. George Patton, Hermann Hesse, Jack London, Rilke, Klee, Kandinsky, Steiner, Mondrian, Sibelius, Lloyd George, Gustav Mahler, Emerson, Thoreau, Ramakrishna, Walt Whitman, Saint Teresa, Joan of Arc, Saint John of the Cross, Boehme, Eckhart, Tolstoi, Dostoevski, Herman Melville, Richard Grossman, Richard Wagner, Robert Browning, Tennyson, Schopenhauer, Nietzsche, Oliver Wendell Holmes, Beethoven, Balzac, Victor Hugo, Thomas Carlyle, Heinrich Heine, Bishop Isadore Balls, Bronson Alcott, Shelley, Hegel, Fichte, Schiller, Schelling, Schlegel, William Blake, Immanuel Kant, Spinoza, Benjamin Franklin (The body of B. F., Printer, Like the Cover of an Old Book, Its Contents Torn Out and Stripped of its Lettering and Gilding, Lies Here Food for Worms, But the Work shall not be Lost, For it Will as He Believed Appear Once More In a New and

More Elegant Edition Revised and Corrected By the Author), Voltaire, Dante, Swedenborg, Leibnitz, Thomas Vaughan, Thomas Traherne, Henry Moore, Giordano Bruno, Paracelsus, Hippolyta, Proclus, Porphyry, Iamblichus, the late Roman emperor Julian, Ammonius Saccas, Origen, Plotinus, Plutarch, Ovid, Lucretius, the Buddha, the authors of the Upanishads and the Vedic Hymns and the *Bhagavad Gita*, the Druid priests, American Indian tribes, Siberians, Patagonians, Peruvians, Eskimos, Aruntas, Tahitians, Okinawans, the people of Madagascar, Zulus, Bantus, Ibos, Yorubas, Freemasons, Theosophists, William Judge, Socrates, Madame Blavatsky, Mahatma Gandhi, Jalal Rumi, Sufis and World-Poles, Friedrich Schleiermacher, the Essenes, Mozart, Arthur Conan Doyle, Somerset Maugham, Jesus of Nazareth, Vivekananda, Amenhotep IV, Bodhidharma, Milarepa, Marpa, Ramana Maharshi, Averroës, Hermes Trismegistus, Domenikos Theotokopoulos, Houston McOstrich, Alexander the Great, Calanus the Gymnosophist, Picasso, Maimonides, Typhus Magee, Ben Hogan, Richard and Hugh of Saint Victor, Sherlock Holmes. But we forget and we forget. Down through the ages we turn away from light!"

The Higher Self

"The Higher Self," which is neither higher nor lower than anything else, was a term of ultimate reference for Shivas. He used it in the manner of the perennial philosophy, to indicate that reality which has been seen and described by mystics and philosophers for thousands of years. It is the *Atman*, the *Brahman*, the *Jiji mu-ge* of Buddhist Philosophy, the Godhead or Fertile Void. To invoke its presence, he sometimes quoted passages from the *Upanishads*, such as these translations I copied from his notes.

One unmoving that is swifter than Mind, That the Gods reach not, for It progresses ever in front. That, standing, passes beyond others as they run . . .

That moves and That moves not; That is far and the same is near; That is within all this and That also is outside all this.

But he who sees everywhere the Self in all existences and all existences in the Self, shrinks not thereafter from anything.

And this from the *Rig Veda*, the first citation in Sri Aurobindo's *Life Divine*.

She follows to the goal of those that are passing on beyond, she is the first in the eternal succession of the dawns that are coming—Usha widens bringing out that which lives, awakening someone who was dead. . . . What is her scope when she harmonises with the dawns that shone out before and those that now must shine? She desires the ancient mornings and fulfills their light; projecting forwards her illumination she enters into communion with the rest that are to come.

Relativity and the Fertile Void

Shivas was explaining a line in his journal which I had asked him about. It read, "Golf is an exercise in perspective: every shot requires that you estimate where you are in relation to the target. Enough golf springs you free."

"Free from what?" I asked.

"From yer attachment to any point. Some part o' yer mind begins to sense the relativity o' things and the fertile void." The "fertile void" had come upon him, as I have said, when he was nineteen and playing golf through those northern summer evenings. He believed that somehow, by some unconscious process, the constant exercise of the sense of perspective required in golf sends a message through to our higher centers that you can never be in the same place twice in relation to the target. Every moment on the course, like every moment in life, is to some degree unique and unrepeatable. And from that realization the mind begins to grope, perhaps unconsciously, for some secure place that never requires a final standpoint in this always shifting world. The mystics have described such a place, or such a no-place, and have called it by names like the Godhead or the Brahman or the Fertile Void.

Such exercises in perspective are a good thing, he said, "for nothing seems satisfying to us short of that. And this Western world is finally getting the message—just before the game is over." Apparently our entire Western culture is learning the lesson in its journey round the globe. It has been forced to change its perspectives so many times.

Not that he was against a sense of duty and doing our work in the world. Far from it. But "part of our human duty is *to bring Being into higher definition* and not save it any more for the Sabbath or the Judgement Day."

Postponement can get to be a disease.

Universal Transparency and a Solid Place to Swing From

Tradition has it that contemplative masters, be they yogis, shamans, Sufis, or Neo-Platonic seers, can read another's mind and heart. As cosmic consciousness develops, the hidden side of things becomes transparent. The deepest Self begins to show itself to itself (*Atman* in Sanskrit is a reflexive pronoun). The world becomes the Net of Jewels in which each jewel reflects every other. We need not be mystics to have glimpsed this possibility, however: how many times have you read your friend or lover in a moment of clarity or high careless embrace? You know you cannot gossip about a friend without his somehow knowing.

Shivas confided to me during our final conversation that a few of his pupils had become so open to hidden influences while developing their game under his tutelage that he had to teach them how to close off and shield themselves again. "Ye must have a solid place to swing from, before ye open up so wide," he said, "otherwise ye'll be swept away." He made a big distinction between "Mind-at-Large," which included all the invisible worlds around you, and the Higher Self. He said that it was wise to know the latter before you opened to the former, otherwise you could drown in the sea of forces and impressions forever enveloping you and pressing to enter. That is the reason for discipline in the contemplative life and for monastery walls to protect you. That is the reason nearly every great teacher has stressed the importance of a healthy body. The old explorers knew what dangers lay in wait once the familiar psychic boundaries had been crossed. Nowadays this wisdom is often forgotten. Many a seeker, opened up and made bold perhaps by LSD or some other plunge to the inner depths, has mistaken each new experience for enlightenment, each hot pleasure for the kiss of God. Moral entropy is often mistaken for nirvana.

"Ye need a solid place to swing from," a place above and beyond these teeming worlds. " 'Tis a thin line," he said, " 'tween the madness of God and the madness of the Devil."

Humans Have Two Sides

or

Dualism Is All Right

Shivas was left-handed. I did not consider it an important fact until I heard about discoveries concerning the distinctive roles of the left and right sides of the brain in mediating different types of mental activity. Shivas also had that disconcerting left eye, focused slightly to the center except when he came back from his trance that morning. Was that eye always watching for messages from the non-verbal hemisphere of his brain (located perhaps on his right side), and was it content to look straight ahead only after he had received some deep inspiration? Then I remembered that he had originally played the game from the left, changing over to conventional right-handedness about the time he reached puberty. (In that he was like Ben Hogan, who had also begun from the deviant side.) Did his muscle memory and golfing unconscious carry all that left-handed perspective still? Was his intuition informed by all those thousands of left-handed shots? (I remembered that Hogan had shifted from a tendency to hook to a deliberate fade when he reached the peak of his game: was he still wrestling with the left-hander in his soul?) I don't have the answers to all these questions, but some things he said make more sense now in the light of recent brain research. For example, he commented on the game's asymmetry and said that it reflected our essentially human imbalance. "The Fall was a fall from the Right," I seem to remember him saying with that sly, hard-to-fathom look he was wont to give me whenever he was making an especially significant remark. "That the game is played from one side always reminds us that we're still lop-sided and incomplete." Indeed, humans are the only animals on the earth whose brain function is asymmetrical: no other creature must wrestle with the angels and demons of speech and elaborate conceptualization.* Mystics have always said that words can be a barrier to enlightenment. The Upanishad says that liberation lies beyond "the golden lid" of thought. Men have long felt this separation from their fuller being as a fall and have told the tragic story in their myths. Golf reflects the Fall, said Shivas, "the fall from the Right."

But the game also shows us a way out. Some of the psychologists studying these things maintain that all contemplative disciplines are "strategies for getting around the left lobe of the brain." They point to the fact that certain gestures used in meditation, the mudras of Hindu-Buddhist practice for example, play on the left-right aspects of life (the "left-hand path," a "left-handed blessing"), that certain ritual proceedings make a big thing out of which way the devotee turns or faces, that the dances of the dervishes turn to the left and then the right. Shivas had said that each golf shot involves a small turn of the body to the left as one comes into the ball (if one plays right-handed) and that this subtle turn has something to do with inspiration. Once again his largely untutored genius had sensed an important connection—with dervish dancing no less! For in those Sufi whirlings one can open to

---

* Such wisdom of the body is there in our language: the word sinister derives from the Latin word for left, and remember that the left side in action connects to the inspired right brain; the word right has meanings to stretch across an entire page of a modern dictionary, all of them pointing to the structuring and proper aligning of life's many aspects in the linear mode of civilized order, e.g., mathematics' right angles, civil and legal rights, what is fitting and desirable, genuine and authentic, straight or perpendicular, ethical and sound, at the right time and right place, etc. Our language is deeply informed by our ever-present two-sidedness.

Mind-at-Large if one turns with attention centered on the heart or inner eye. That is not unlike the centered turnings of golf, or so at least our philosopher of the links suspected.*

The left-right dimension of the game is also involved in the relationship between voluntary and involuntary controls. All skill involves a certain measure of spontaneity and unconscious functioning: no one can create beauty, be it in a work of art or on a golfing links, unless he has both disciplined control and the ability to let go to the sudden glimmer. In following the leadings of the "inner eye" while visualizing a shot or sensing what club to use, one must draw upon all the unconscious stores of learning one possesses. We all know that. We all know that we could never plan each shot exactly without that immediate tacit knowing which comes from immersion in the game over years and decades. Every shot has a conscious component and an unconscious one, a voluntary control and one that is involuntary. To know how to strike the balance is the very essence of golfing skill. The greatest champions, while having grooved swings to envy, come up with surprises that astound us. They pull off the unbelievable shot in the midst of contingencies too numerous to calculate ever. How else to account for Shivas's hole-in-one that night on the thirteenth hole? Or, if modesty allows me, my own shot there that afternoon? One of the beauties of sport is the inspirational heart-stopping move that reminds us of possibilities yet unguessed.

Inspiration and spontaneity must be given their place if any game is to be mastered and enjoyed. But, alas, there is a tendency in many golfers to repress all wellings from within and all the delicate leadings in their devotion to some steely program of the will.

Not only must one learn how to strike a fine balance between the disciplined and the inspired, but one must know

---

* Of course, the golf swing is an incomplete dervish turn. Obviously this aspect of the game needs more research.

when to quit, said Shivas, "and even when to collapse. . . . There is a time for lettin' the bottom drop out," he said, "for forgettin' yer score entirely, for forgettin' yer mental tricks and devices, for just swingin' any ol' way ye please." If we don't do this from time to time, he said, "our game goes kaflooey" anyway. Indeed if you were an absolute perfectionist on the links, if you could not stand to see a single bad score on your handicap card, you would never have come as far as you have with the game. When you allow yourself to fail on the links, the golfing unconscious learns the lessons which such unwindings teach. Perhaps the left and right sides of your brain are readjusting their marriage, perhaps some tangle in the nerveways of the autonomic system is shaking itself out; whatever the specifics of this "positive disintegration," renewal may be on the way. "One of the joys of self-knowledge," say the journal notes, "is the increasing sense one gets of the soul's wise rhythms."

The process is trying to work all the time, even when we are unaware or refusing assent. Then collapse may force itself upon us. Gambling, he said, is one unconscious way of tempting collapse, a "positive disintegration" that doesn't renew. It is a way of calling in the inexorable powers of chance to ape the experience of being overwhelmed. To lose a bundle brings secret relief, I know from my own experience and that of certain relatives who carry the propensity. (My brother, for example, had already lost the family's grand piano when he was fourteen: I will never forget the astonishment on my parents' faces when a Bekins van moved up to the house and the movers announced they were taking it away.) But gambling is not the only way of escaping through the back door of our psyche, there are endless ways of downward transcendence and dark dissolution. Murder, conspiracy, drugs, the orgy: we have only to read the daily newspaper to see such collapse all around us. And there will be more. I do not think I am stretching a point when I say that all of these are ways to effect the release our psyche periodically needs.

There are various kinds of transcendence. Some lead to God and others to the Reign of Hell on earth.

But golf is still our business. For on the links there are ways to give way gracefully, to collapse with grace under that pressure from within. With Shivas I did it and shot a 34 to boot. It can be done even while shooting your loveliest golf, especially if you follow true gravity's subtle leading.

"The Fall had its place and always will," might be a good line from the notes to end this section with, "for everything human has two sides."

Even Dualism is all right in his plural theology.

His Ideal

A few of my friends have asked me to explain in some clear and fundamental way just what it was that Shivas Irons was finally hoping for. What is his *ideal?* they sometimes ask. George Leonard, with whom I share leadings like these more than I do with any other living person, has asked me time and again to characterize the goal my golfing teacher held up for us. It has been a difficult question to answer, for there is a certain amorphous and undefinable quality to his teaching. When I come to putting it down on paper, I have a feeling that I am forcing his vision; that no matter how I state the goal he would set, there is something left over that words will always leave out. So having warned you that this is the case, I will now proceed to lay out some first thoughts about the High Ideal of Shivas Irons (with all credit to Seamus Mac-Duff) concerning the Way We Should and Someday Will Be in This Fallen but All-Promising World of Ours.

"The world's a koan," he assured me just before I left, "a koan from the very beginnin' and gettin' worse day by day." A koan, as you probably know, is the paradox-invoking question Zen masters give their students to open up their minds; a famous one asks, "Before your parents were, what is your original face?" It is intended to reveal the Buddha-Mind underlying all the seeming paradoxes of our ordinary existence. Shivas believed that life presented us with koans every day, that if we approached them with an open, ready spirit the whole world turned to Zen training and successive revelation, that if we turned away they reappeared like Hydra heads. There is no escaping the paradoxes life presents us with; we can only choose whether to embrace or escape them.

The sense of paradox is growing more intense as human awareness develops and people crowd together around the globe; that is what he was referring to when he said it was "getting worse day by day."

"So many Gods and moralities now, so many logics and geometries, so many ways to see the world, so many ideas about running a family," his notes lament. "The Twentieth Century itself is a *koan*."

The twentieth century as *koan*! The thought has obsessed me ever since I read it there, in Burningbush, fifteen years ago. It has set me thinking about the way our knowledge and art have turned the world into a roller coaster and a prism: how anthropology has revealed a thousand ethical codes and endless variety of sexual practice, how the study of families all over the earth has given support to a thousand deviant experiments in the U.S.A.; how Freud has shown us as much deviance and urge to break free in the psyche of the solid American citizen; how while this undermining of taboo is taking place, the intellect's certainties are giving way —to endless systems of logic and geometry, to playful models of the nature of matter, to the strong solvent of linguistic and philosophic analysis, to theologies that God is dead; how, while our moral and philosophical certitudes are dissolving, the artist breaks our perceptions down—into cubes, circles, and squares, into points of light and toilet seats, into the very vibrations of our retinal nerves, showing us once and for all that distance is nowhere fundamentally proper, that there is no *right* place to stand any more (for a cup is a cup in its middle or its edge, from a foot away or underneath a garbage can—a cup and the moon can look the same once you look more closely), even sound fragments as melody and harmony go into microscopes and magnifications of sense and come out like Stockhausen; how, while our morals and beliefs and perceptions proliferate, the commonalities of a given day take on a melting surrealistic uncertainty and our trusted friends and lovers are filled with sudden new intensities and challenge us in the middle of the night (the newspapers are full of it, so are the movies and the books and conspiracies all around); everywhere our certainties, our ideals and beliefs and most familiar perceptions are ripped away like our very own flesh, as if our souls were being skinned alive. Yes, there is no denying it, the twentieth century is a koan, pressing us to paradox until we cry uncle. When I hear *Hare Krishna* on the streets of the city I hear my own impulse to surrender forever to the One beyond all these incertitudes. At times I imagine our entire nation breaking into such a cry, going back to Jesus or Buddha or Muhammad—or finding a center in violence or oblivion self-induced. For there is no escaping the growing pressure. The koan is upon us with a vise-like grip and it is squeezing harder every day.

"A chameleon on a tartan plaid, that was the way it felt," said Shivas, describing his own early state. He was turning seventeen ways at once until the spirit broke through with an image of epilepsy and his body dismembered. His painful yet joyous reconstruction of character began that summer in Burningbush after the koan had finally exploded—I have already told you the story as I know it. Through primitive group therapy with members of the club, through years of study, meditation, golf in true gravity, and countless good deeds to his friends he had come to the glowing ever-adventurous state I found him in. He was well beyond despair and fragmentation by then.

I open a consideration of his "ideal" with these reflections because I think they point to the state and attitude he would bring us to. For, as he put it, "there is always a Body beyond our little body, arms to hold us, new eyes to see, a larger being waiting here closer than our physical skin." There is a deeper self that thrives on the craziness of this teeming world, that "sees every breakdown as an opening to the original crazy shimmering dance, to the eternal explosion of the sun in the night, to the floating worlds all around."

His ideal would have us know this Body and this Dance, would have us live in it while playing golf and singing ballads and talking to our friends; yes, and even while we are trying to pass it on to others.

A Postscript:
The Dance of Shiva

In South India, not far from Madras and Pondicherry, lies the Temple of Chidambaram, known to many as the original home of Natarajan, the dancing Shiva. The temple there is like a canyon-fort, with great walls enclosing smaller temples of varying shapes and sizes, all of them passageways to different parts of Shiva's body. One without windows is black as night and houses the God's *akashic*, or etheric *Lingam*: in its dark recess Hindu women cover the black and tapering stone with melted butter, stroking it slowly until its shape is worn smooth. Another houses the great bell, which is struck to announce disappearances and renewals of the God. Around the compound there is a corridor with a thousand pillars, and near its southern gate there stands the pavilion with the famous figure. When the pavilion doors are open you can see the King of Dancers from any point—dancing on a pyramid of gods and demons in a prefiguration of His dance to bring the world down and end the cosmic cycle.

I visited the temple while I was at the Aurobindo ashram near the end of my journey around the world, passing through the outer gates in the wake of an American sadhu with orange robes and a devastating smile who said it had come to him in a dream that he should bring me here. The moment I crossed the threshold I felt the presence of the God. Not the excitement of anticipation merely or the strangeness of the place, but the overwhelming presence of

Shiva, as tangible as the drum rolls and basso chanting one heard in the distance.

We walked in silence around the temple compound, past the candelit cave which housed the *Lingam* (women chanting as they rubbed its sides, being entered by its etheric substance for ether is the medium of sound, and this is its *Lingam*), past the temple bell, and smaller passages that showed you Shiva's many faces, down the thousand-pillared corridor to the edge of a crowd pressing round the dancing figure. Its flying arms and legs were perfect poise. It was glowing as if lit from within.

Ceremonies were beginning and the Brahmin priests of Tamilnad were seated around the statue in ascending banks, chanting Sanskrit mantras with a ringing power and hard, insistent beat—a beat to open nerveways of the densest mind, no one, no part to be left behind in this culminating act of worship. Then the sliding doors slammed shut. The God had disappeared.

The crowd pressed closer, and for a moment I was lost in the wavering space. Then the doors slid back. The God was covered high with flowers, a mountain of petals and blossoms where the statue had been, and the Sanskrit chant began to swell, hint of frenzy ordered by the mantra-beat, every white-robed figure bobbing now with growing passion.

They began to stroke the flowers away, to unveil Natarajan, the King of Dancers. Then the doors slammed shut.

Then opened to show a pile of rice, Shiva in the food of India.

Seven times the God was covered and revealed—Natarajan at the center of all the elements, dancing even in glowing stone. Each time the doors swung open the great bell rang and those hundreds in the pressing crowd saw Shiva at the heart of things.

In flowers, rice, bread, and stone; the Dance. His arms and legs the tendrils of exploding worlds, his eyes eternal stillness, his smile the ecstasy. The Dance was at the heart of every atom.

A Bibliography for the Reconstructed Golfer

Assagioli, Roberto. *Psychosynthesis: A Manual of Principles and Techniques*. New York: The Viking Press, Compass Books, 1971.

Aurobindo, Sri. *The Life Divine*. New York: India Library Society, 1949.

——. *The Synthesis of Yoga*. Pondicherry: Sri Aurobindo Ashram Press, 1955.

Satprem. *Sri Aurobindo or The Adventure of Consciousness*. New York: India Library Society, 1964.

Carlyle, Thomas. *Sartor Resartus, The Life and Opinions of Herr Teufelsdröckh*. New York: The Odyssey Press, 1937.

Gurney, Edmund. *Phantasms of the Living*. Gainesville, Fla: Scholars' Facsimiles & Reprints. (In two volumes). 1886 & 1970.

Kirkaldy, Andra. *My Fifty Years of Golf: Memories*. London: T. Fisher Unwin Ltd., 1921.

Leonard, George B. *The Transformation*. Los Angeles: Jeremy P. Tarcher. 1986.

Myers, Frederic. *Human Personality and Its Survival of Bodily Death*. New York: Longmans, Green & Co. (In two volumes). 1903 & 1954.

MacDuff, Seamus. *The Logarithms of the Just, Being First Notes for a Physics of the Spirit*. (Unpublished manuscript.)

THE SHIVAS IRONS SOCIETY

The SHIVAS IRONS SOCIETY is a non-profit corporation organized to further the pleasure of golf and to explore its many mysteries. It is comprised of individuals who share a common love for the game and an admiration of those qualities of body and soul exemplified by the powerful and enigmatic character for which it is named.

Among the purposes of the SOCIETY are the fostering of education through golf, the support of golf related charitable activities, the celebration of the beauty and virtues of the game, and the honoring of its history and Scottish roots. The SOCIETY organizes and sponsors seminars, clinics, and conferences to promote its various purposes. The SOCIETY also publishes a newsletter to inform the membership of its activities and to provide a forum for the sharing of ideas.

For membership or other information write:

The Shivas Irons Society
Post Office Box 222339
Carmel, CA 93922-2339

or FAX: *408-626-6701*